How to Plan Your African-American Family Reunion

HOW TO PLAN YOUR
AFRICAN-AMERICAN
FAMILY REUNION

Krystal G. Williams

Citadel Press
Kensington Publishing Corp.
www.kensingtonbooks.com

CITADEL PRESS books are published by

Kensington Publishing Corp.
850 Third Avenue
New York, NY 10022

First printing 2000

10 9 8 7 6 5 4 3 2 1

Printed in the United States of America

ISBN 0-8065-2097-3

Cataloging data for this publication can be obtained from the Library of
Congress.

CONTENTS

INTRODUCTION

My grandmother has a special room she calls "*the front room.*" In this room are all of her most prized possesions carefully arranged and displayed for company to see. Among the possessions most proudly and prominently displayed are the family photographs. Shelf after shelf is lined with picture frames. Some are elaborate frames trimmed in gold. Some are simple frames made of wood. On other shelves, photo album after photo album contain the faces of all my relatives. Some I know and love; some I do not know or have not met, yet still love. I love these people because all are tied to me, and I am tied to them by an extraordinary bond known as family.

WHAT IS A FAMILY?

According to the tenth edition of Merriam Webster's Collegiate Dictionary, a family is a group of individuals living under one roof and usually under one head—a household. However, the face of the family is ever changing. Where we used to think of a traditional, nuclear family as mother, father, and children, we must now acknowledge the advent of single-parent families; extended families in which an aunt, uncle, or grandmother is the head of the family; and foster families.

Some believe a family that does not have all of the traditional elements in place is bound for destruction. Grim statistics cited by experts who monitor American society draw a distinct correlation between the absence of a mother or father in the home and the eventual breakdown of the African-American family. We hear about it all the time on the news. We cannot turn on the television, listen to the radio, or pick up a newspaper without hearing how poorly the African-American family is faring.

According to an article posted by the U.S. Department of Commerce, Economics, and Statistics Administration, the 1990 census estimated that 55 percent of African-American children living in metropolitan areas (cities such as New York or Atlanta) lived in single-parent households. The growth of single-parent families (an alarming number of which are begun by teenaged girls) has been blamed on the rising costs of welfare and public assistance.

In a bulletin, which discusses an overview of youth gangs in America, the U.S. Department of Justice reports, "The United States has seen rapid proliferation of young gangs since 1990. During this period," the report continues, "the number of cities with gang problems increased from an estimated 286 jurisdictions with more than 2,000 gangs and nearly 100,000 gang members to about 4,800 jurisdictions with more than 31,000 gangs and approximately 846,000 gang members in 1996." According to this same bulletin, the ethnicity of gang members is reported as 48 percent African-American.

If we heed these frightening statistics about our families, about our children, we can only come to the conclusion that we are losing an entire generation to poverty, violence, and ignorance. The word *ignorance* sounds harsh. However, if we all knew, understood, and imitated the resilient and resourceful nature of our ancestors, we wouldn't throw up our hands so easily and give up our beseiged families.

African-Americans are survivors. History, which is a collection of life experiences, has told the story. Whether during the month of February (Black History Month) or all year long, we've learned to embrace our history, heritage, and culture. We've learned how our ancestors faced incredible odds from disease to forced labor as well as forced separation from the new families they adapted and adopted in this country.

Even after African-Americans were freed from legalized slavery through a series of legal edicts and constitutional amendments, our ancestors still faced overwhelming odds. Hatred and bigotry, legalized segregation, and unpunished crimes drove our ancestors from our rural, agricultural beginnings on southern plantations to points north and west.

Our ancestors risked their lives to learn to read, receive the right to vote, and contribute to building this nation. With tenacity and faith, we became pioneers and explorers, farmers and storekeepers. We became lawyers and laymen, politicians and preachers. All I have to do is look at the accomplishments of my own family to know what African-Americans in general are capable of achieving.

Though my family lives in all points on the globe, we are forever connected by our love for one another. The power of this bond was made crystal clear to me one afternoon, in the spring of 1990 after the birth of my first child. At that point, I was now teasingly considered an adult, and could sit in my grandmother's front room without other "adults" making sure that I didn't knock over a knickknack or puncture a picture with my childhood games.

As I sat, rocking my child and telling her how lucky she was to be born into such a large, loving family, my eyes strayed to a photograph of my mother when she was my age. Our resemblance was amusing—and amazing. Despite the old-fashioned hairstyle and the funky, retro 1960's psychedelic clothes, I saw my face in hers. We had the same wide, brown eyes, the same quick smile.

Searching for more photographs, I found a picture of my grandmother in the 1930's when she was about my mother's age. I was startled how much my grandmother way back then looked like my mother looks now! That meant, in some way, I looked like my grandmother, too.

Finally, when I looked at the photograph of my great-grandmother hanging on the wall, and realized how much my grandmother looked like my great-grandmother, the true meaning of my family and my African-American heritage dawned on me.

I had never met my great-grandmother, yet I am connected to her by more than blood or shared physical features. But, it also makes me wonder what else I have in common with the family members I have never met.

Wanting to know more about my family, to make the connection between the past and present, is one of the main reasons I am so enthusiastic about planning and participating in family reunions. Yet, it is not enough to learn about the success stories of the past. We must use our family reunions to encourage and uplift the success stories of our future generations. In between the fun and the food, the picnics and the parties, take a moment to embrace, educate, and encourage.

HOW TO PLAN YOUR AFRICAN-AMERICAN FAMILY REUNION

1

Is This Job
Right for You?

There are three kinds of people in the world:
Those who make things happen.
Those who watch things happen.
Those who wonder what happened.

—UNKNOWN

W hat kind of person are you? Are you a watcher? Or are you a doer? If you've picked up this book, chances are that you are a doer—or want to be. The idea of planning your family reunion appeals to you. But, you're not sure where to start.

TAKING THE FIRST STEP

Making the commitment to your extended family may be the hardest part about planning a family reunion. You will not only be contacting the people who are near and dear to your heart, you will also be reaching out to people who may be virtual strangers to you. Don't forget you will be committing precious time, hard-earned money, and valuable property, such as family heirlooms to put on display for this event.

There are so many details to consider, so many pieces that must be put into place for a family reunion to go smoothly. A thousand questions may run through your mind. Where should the reunion be held? Should you plan a one-day reunion or one that lasts several days? How do you track down long-lost relatives? How do you order T-shirts? Should you hire a photographer or take your own pictures?

The thought of pulling together a family reunion may seem a little overwhelming—whether your family is small and lives close together or whether your family numbers in the thousands and is widely scattered. In fact, many reunion organizers begin planning their reunion as early as a year before the reunion date. This reunion planner will give you some guidelines to help make the yearlong task more manageable. It will also give you several creative starting point ideas to help make your reunion more memorable.

KEEPING THE MOMENTUM GOING

As you start to plan and watch the fruits of your labor blossom, there may be times when you wonder whether your efforts are appreciated. If you start to feel that way, stop! Stop and consider why you are doing this. Maybe it's because you haven't seen members of your family in a long time or maybe your family has always held reunions and now the duty of planning them has fallen to you. Whatever the reason, accept the responsibility of drawing your family together as a labor of love—the same labor of love that brought you into this world.

Your family gave you life. A family reunion celebrates life by paying homage to the ones who came before you and by uplifting the ones who have come after you.

It's tough planning a family reunion. In addition to the day-to-day activities you tackle, such as work, family, and church, there is only so much of you to give. Whenever you start to queston your reasons for doing this, go to your family photo albums and look for a picture of the youngest member of your family. Then, search for a photo of the oldest member of your family. Place them side by side. What similarities do you note? Maybe it's in the shape of the nose or the color of their eyes. Maybe they have the same last name. Maybe they share similar interests. The answers to these questions will remind you that the people in those pictures are related to you. They are your family.

Also ask yourself what differences you see. These differences help make them unique. We can all learn and benefit by celebrating our differences, whether we are copper-toned or obsidian, doctors or dockworkers. The people in these photographs are bound together by blood. Joining them at a family reunion that you have had the privilege of planning or helped to plan binds them together by love. And love is a powerful motivator.

The job of planning your family reunion is not thankless. It's selfless. It is a gift of love that will be appreciated for generations to come. Through your efforts, you help bring knowledge to the next generation that could never be found in history books.

BRINGING IT ON HOME

Remember, as you are planning your reunion, that there are no wrong or right ways to do it. All that really matters is that you have the desire and the commitment to follow through. As you go through the guidelines of this planner, remember that some ideas may work for you. Some may not. Be adventuresome. Here's your chance to show off the depth of creativity that has carried us through the ages. Put on your thinking cap and your running shoes, and let's get this party started.

2

GETTING STARTED

Deal with yourself as an individual worthy of respect,
and make everyone else deal with you the same way.

— NIKKI GIOVANNI

SINGLE-PERSON ORGANIZER

Before you take that first step toward organizing your reunion, take a moment to think about how you work best. Planning a reunion is a rewarding but demanding opportunity. Do you enjoy making decisions? Do you look forward to facing challenges? If problem solving and being the "go-to person" doesn't present a problem to you, then you will thrive acting as a single-person organizer.

The single-person planner must be many things to many people—communicator, investigator, treasurer, and sometimes referee. A single-person organizer has to be extremely organized, detail-oriented, and thoroughly committed to the task of pulling together every aspect of the family reunion. Otherwise, even with the best intentions, plans will remain simply plans—unfulfilled dreams of what could have been.

Although you are the one organizing the reunion, don't think that you have to do everything yourself. You can't be in two places at the same time. If you try to do it all yourself, you'll run yourself ragged. When the reunion day actually arrives, you won't have any energy to participate. Also, since there are so many details of which to keep track, it may be easy to overlook items.

Get friends and family to help you with the planning and carrying out the reunion activities. The more relatives you get involved, the greater the interest in the occasion. When you involve relatives in the planning, they have a greater personal stake in the reunion's success. The more people are interested in the reunion, the higher the attendance will be. On the practical side, the more people that attend the family reunion, the greater the contribution to the reunion funds.

Even though the availability of funds makes the difference in the type of reunion that you have, it should not be the only reason you want to invite all of your relatives. The more people that attend the reunion, the greater the possibility for fun! After all, a reunion is a time for celebrating.

As the single-person organizer, think of yourself as the point of a pyramid. You are at the top. You are the main point of contact when coordinating this event. All final decisions come through you. The family and friends who help you are the base of the pyramid; they support your efforts. However, being a single-person organizer doesn't mean that you are the dictator. Your job is not to issue commands or make demands. Your job is to provide the vision and the drive behind the family reunion. The single-person organizer relies on the expertise and the enthusiasm of the people helping to make the reunion planning go smoothly. Without a solid support structure, the effort will crumble. Share the responsibilities as well as the rewards.

An Example of a Single-Person Organizer

Orlean Dorsey was a single-person planner. Orlean is a data administrator for a multinational computer company. As a data administrator, his job is to define how information is stored. He makes sure that information is spread and used consistently throughout the company. His communication skills came in very handy when he planned his family reunions.

Having that much professional responsibility didn't necessarily grant him instant respect by his family members. Since he was named after his father, his family affectionately knows Orlean as "Junior." In fact, Orlean sheepishly admits, "When I first started calling everybody to discuss putting together a family reunion, I would use my real name. My relatives would say, 'Orlean? Orlean, who?' and I would have to admit, 'It's Junior.' Only then would people listen to me and some of my ideas."

Orlean knows his way around a family reunion. Both sides of his family hold them often and he has planned or coordinated three of his own.

Committee Planning

Are you the sociable type? Does the idea of sharing the responsibility and the praise appeal to you? Do you work best when you are part of a larger group? Then perhaps you would be more creative working as part of a committee.

Some family reunion organizers find it easier to form a committee to plan their reunion. If the family is large enough or the events are elaborate, some families also organize subcommittees. The subcommittees determine what tasks need to be performed and who will carry them out. The following are some sample family reunion planning committees:

- Budget Committee: raises and manages the funds that will pay for the reunion events. Managing the funds includes keeping track of family dues, opening bank accounts to hold the funds that pay for events and activities, and paying bills.

- Correspondence Committee: contacts relatives to keep them informed of reunion activities. This committee keeps all names and addresses up to date.

- Emergency Aid Committee: provides assistance in the event of an emergency. Committee members should know the basics of first aid and cardiopulmonary resucitation (CPR).

- Family History Committee: collects family photos, researches the family genealogy, and creates the family tree.

- Food Committee: arranges all of the meals during the reunion. If meals are catered, the food committee researches and hires the caterer. If relatives supply meals, this committee organizes who will bring which dishes.

- Program Committee: plans and coordinates the events and activities that will be held during the reunion. For example, if you plan to have a guest speaker, the program committee ensures that the speaker is at the appointed place at the appointed time.

- Reunion Site Committee: investigates the possible locations for hosting the family reunion, such as which city. This committee also researches the hotels, restaurants, and picnic sites.

- Transportation Committee: provides transportation to and from sites where needed. The volunteers for this committee must have clean driving records, dependable vehicles, and adequate liability insurance to cover themselves and passengers in the event of an accident.

For effective planning, the family reunion committee should work as a true organization electing officers for such positions as president, vice president, secretary, treasurer, and historian. You may not need all of these committees to help plan your family reunion. Breaking up tasks makes it easier to get jobs done but it also means that there are more people to try to coordinate. Some of these committees can be combined or eliminated depending on the type of reunion that you want. Decide what works well for you.

Examples of Committee-Based Planners

Mary Jane Duncan-Livingston, known as "Libby" to her coworkers, is a surgical nurse, specializing in elective and plastic surgery. She has served as both the vice president and treasurer of her reunion planning committee. She has organized each of her family reunions for more than a decade. In 1985, when she first began the effort to start up the tradition of a family reunion, only two people supported the bulk of the reunion events, helped to coordinate, fund, and clean up after a reunion that lasted for four days and drew more than a hundred people. All of the time and experience she's had planning reunions has given her this one pearl of wisdom: "With so much to do to plan your reunion, and the growing fear that there is so little time to do it, don't be afraid to ask for help. Just because you're the one planning the reunion doesn't mean that you have to do everything all by yourself."

Mal J. Wiley, known as "Sonny" to his friends and family, is vice president and director of a nonprofit organization that owns a housing complex for the elderly and handicapped. Before that, he was a sergeant detective for the Austin, Texas, police department.

When it comes to planning his family reunion, Mal likes a touch of the unconventional. He likes to plan reunion sites that are interesting and off-beat. For his 1997 family reunion, Mal used a convenient recreational facility that just happened to be maintained by the Huntsville, Texas, prison system.

Donna White is a production administrator for a technical writing–consulting services company. One of her many jobs involves making certain that technical documents are printed and delivered on time so that they can be packaged with their products. Donna is a very organized, detail-oriented team player. She can't do her job unless she works hand in hand with all of the various people who develop, edit, approve, and print the documentation.

When it comes to making sure that all of the pieces are pulled together at the right time, "Sometimes," Donna admits, "you've got to get tough with people. That doesn't mean getting nasty. But you can be firm and get your point across." That advice also applies to organizing family reunions.

Donna is the mother of two very active children. She is also an active member of her church. She has either organized or participated in at least five family reunions.

Valerie Merlett is a technical-support specialist for a multinational computer company. Her duties include providing answers to customers' questions or soothing tensions when a customer is dissatisfied. Her ability to research information in order to provide answers and to remain calm in the face of an irate customer gives her some necessary skills when planning her family's reunion. She is also a mother of two. Juggling career and family, Valerie demonstrates a reunion planner's most advantageous trait—the ability to tackle multiple tasks at once.

When problems crop up, Valerie is one of the first to pitch in with a "let's get it resolved" attitude.

VOLUNTEERS

The single-person organizer cannot perform all of the duties of reunion planning. Even committee-based planners must look to outside help to complete the many tasks involved with orchestrating a family reunion. Though many of your family members may express an interest in helping out with the reunion plans, sometimes conflicts prevent those eager relatives from following through with their commitments. You will find that a core group of volunteers will always be available to pitch in when needed. These are the unsung heroes that help us run the errands, watch the children, and lend the utensils that help make the reunion-planning process appear smooth and effortless.

COMMITTEE MEETINGS

Once you have an idea of who you will have helping you with planning the reunion, you can decide how often to meet. This will be dictated by how easy it is for family members to get together. Consider your busy schedules and how closely you live together. If you have committee members who are out of the state, you will not be able to meet as often as you would if you lived closely together.

Once you decide who is on a committee, either by volunteers or conscription, you can determine when the best time is to meet. Set a specific time, place, and location, and communicate that information to all of the committee members. Once you do meet, make it a fun and productive event so that committee members maintain their enthusiasm and their commitment.

I usually start my committee meetings with a small prayer of thanks or a moment of silence so we can give thanks in our own special way. This reminds us that though we are here to plan a good time and to have a good time, we are getting together for a serious reason.

In the beginning planning phase, you may only think it necessary to meet once a month or every two months. As the reunion date draws nearer, you should plan on meeting more often to work out any details. You should definitely meet the week of the reunion. This is when many of the last-minute details are put into place.

Committee Meeting Points to Cover

Before you jump into the task of planning a reunion, you need some idea or some direction in which to take the plans. For the first committee meeting, start by discussing and answering some of these questions.

- How extensive should the reunion be, a one-day event or a weekend affair?

- When should you host the reunion? Is the time of the year a factor?

- How many family members should be invited?

- Should the reunion be for the grandmother's side of the family, or the grandfather's? Or combined?

- Should the reunion be centered around a theme?

- What, if any, should be the budget limit?

You may not be able to answer all of these questions with the first meeting, but the issues should definitely be raised. As you come up with responses, keep accurate notes and at future meetings, recap the previous meeting's decisions to give you a sense of progress.

Ensuring Our Future

One of the reasons for holding a family reunion is so that we can pay tribute to those who came before us. It is important that we do not forget the lessons of the past. The suffering and the successes of our ancestors have given us the knowledge and the strength we must have to survive the future.

While family reunions are a time to remember the past, they also allow us to look forward to the future. By involving the younger generation in planning the reunions, we pass on the pride of our heritage. In between the hugs and the kisses, the laughter and the games, the food and the photographs, we must make certain that our young people understand the importance of why we are gathering.

Rickeshia Givens, a fifth grader, and her cousin, RaVen Livingston, a third grader (who also happens to be my daughter), gave me some valuable insight on planning a reunion from the younger generation's point of view. When planning a family reunion, we sometimes get so caught up in researching names from the past, that we sometimes forget to look ahead to our future.

When planning reunions, make sure to get input from the younger generation. What type of music do they like? What type of games do they enjoy? How long should you hold certain events, such as family meetings, before you lose the interest of these active minds?

Rickeshia and RaVen were very open about what about their family reunions was stale and boring and what was, in their words, "Da Bomb!"

Planning for Future Reunions

Once you have planned one successful reunion, you are likely brimming with ideas for the next reunion which raises the question—when should the next reunion occur? Some families hold reunions every year. In the beginning, holding a reunion that often builds excitement and participation. As you hold more reunions and the word gets out, you build a following. Also, the planning gets easier as you grow more familiar with the planning process. Holding a family reunion every year also gives you more opportunities for different families to host the reunion in their home state. This keeps the reunion fresh and exciting—new scenery, new reunion planning styles.

Some families chose to alternate their reunions to every other year. This gives them the chance to use their vacations in the off-reunion year to make other plans. Also, if you plan the same type of reunions year after year, family members may experience a feeling of "been there, done that." As a result, attendance slacks off.

Whichever method you decide, every year, every other year, or even every three years, be consistent. You build a better following when family members know what to expect and plan accordingly.

3

MAKING A SCHEDULE

I work late.
Keep the whole world running . . .
—"WORKER'S SONG" BY MAYA ANGELOU

F amily reunions vary in size and length. They can be as simple as a one-day get-together. Or more elaborate—with events spanning several days. Planning for either type of family reunion takes coordination. For example, you don't want the T-shirts you ordered for the reunion arriving one week after the fact. Knowing what has to be in place and when is crucial to the success of any event.

To make tasks more manageable, break up the reunion-planning effort into these distinct phases.

● Before-reunion plans: Events and activities that should be put into place well in advance of the family reunion.

● Reunion event plans: Activities that make up the family reunion, such as picnics, banquets, fashion shows, and family meetings.

● After-reunion plans: Events that will close out the family reunion, such as clean-up detail, closing of accounts, preparations for the next reunion.

16

Once you have a clear idea of how tasks should be grouped, then you can begin figuring out the details of what has to happen. This sample one-year schedule gives you an idea of when to start working on the elements of your reunion.

Date	Events	Helpful Hints
One year ahead	Start contacting family members (gathering names, addresses, etc.).	Contact family members as soon as possible. It is important to get three or four representatives that can help collect addresses, especially since some family members move often.
	Send out surveys (what kind of reunion to have, preferences for music, food, etc.).	If you haven't done so already, be sure to ask how much family members are willing to pay.
	Form committees.	
	Collect seed money.	
	Select a date and location.	
	Send out first newsletter.	The first newsletter should cover all the details such as the date and location of the reunion. You should also solicit ideas for T-shirt designs.

Date	Events	Helpful Hints
Nine months ahead	Open a bank account.	At any earlier point, it may be too soon to open a bank account, unless you can find an institution that doesn't charge a maintenance fee and perhaps pays interest on a small balance.
		Some families have had the same bank account open for years. They keep an account in which adult family members automatically deposit a set amount (usually about $10 a month or $120 a year). This money is used to offset the cost of the family reunion. It can also be used to help another family member experiencing hardship, or to pay a scholarship for a promising college student within the family.
	Send out early notice with preliminary details (where and when).	
	Start holding fund-raisers.	
	Start collecting family dues.	
	Send second family newsletter.	
	Research items for keepsakes.	

Date	Events	Helpful Hints
	Research hotel rates, transportation, and the cost of reserving recreation areas.	
	Make final decisions on location, date, etc. (assuming that the reunion will be held the following summer).	
	Make group travel arrangements twenty-one days to six months in advance.	Most airlines will not book flights twelve months in advance.
Six months ahead	Send third family newsletter.	
	Continue fund-raisers.	
	Send out formal invitations or follow-up letters.	
	Solicit park permits (where needed).	
	Reserve block of hotel rooms.	
	Line up entertainment, guest speakers.	If you are paying someone, be sure to have a signed contract.
	Order keepsakes.	Give the vendors a deadline of at least two weeks in advance of the event, allow more time for special circumstances, such as traveling out of state.

Date	Events	Helpful Hints
Three months ahead	Contact mayor's office or local politician for proclamation letter.	A good keepsake is a city proclamation. To get one commemorating your event, apply at the Mayor's office at least two months in advance.
	Send out final family newsletter or reminder notices.	Take advantage of the final newsletter to really "hype-up" the event. Talk about how great it will be and try to stimulate interest in those who aren't planning on coming. The final newsletter is equivalent to a Super Bowl.
	Purchase non-perishables (plates, silverware, decorations).	If someone has a deep freezer it may be a good idea to start purchasing meats at this time. More often than not, the demand for ribs and brisket goes up during the warmer months, thus driving the prices up slightly. What my family does is keep an eye open for special prices on these items and stay ready to buy when an exceptionally good deal comes along.
	Arrange for security, trash receptacles, etc.	Don't forget the portable potty if restrooms are not readily available.

Date	Events	Helpful Hints
Two weeks before event	Have a "dress rehearsal." Make sure everyone is aware of his or her assignments and try to anticipate things that may not go as planned.	
	Program committee should purchase games, prizes, etc.	All committees should make final purchases at this time, then have expenses turned in a week before. That way you have a good idea of how well you are doing against your budget.
Week of the event	Final meeting of all committees to discuss any outstanding items.	
	Souvenir booklets should be available within a week of the event.	
One month after the event	Send a follow-up newsletter. In it summarize the events that took place (I try to get a report from one of the kid's perspective, from the perspective of one of the senior adults, and one or two other comments). Also, use this newsletter to start hyping the next reunion. A good selling point is to account for all the funds in either this newsletter or the souvenir booklet.	

* * * * *

4

GETTING A HEAD COUNT

*Taped to the wall . . . are 47 pictures: 47 black
faces: my father, mother, grandmothers (1 dead),
grandfathers (both dead), brothers, sister, uncles,
aunts, cousins (1st and 2nd) nieces, and nephews*
        —"THE IDEA OF ANCESTRY" BY ETHERIDGE KNIGHT

Ancestry. Who came before us? Who paved the way
for us? Who loved us and supported us? Who gave
us those kicks in the pants when we needed that extra,
added incentive to keep going? A family reunion lets us
honor the memories of our forebearers.

Legacy. Who will come after us? Who are our future
leaders? Who will be responsible for maintaining the traditions of the past? Who are the ones responsible for breathing new life and new energy into the family by starting new
traditions? A family reunion lets us celebrate and encourage
the efforts of our young ones.

That is why each and every family member, young and
old, is vital to the success of any family reunion. As you plan
your reunion, keep in mind that you want to hold it at a
time and a location so you can get as much participation as
you can. Knowing how many people to expect affects every
decision that follows in the planning of your reunion. For

example, if you're planning to have a catered meal, you'll need an accurate head count to ensure that there will be plenty of food for everyone. Or, if you are ordering keepsakes such as T-shirts, you'll need to have an accurate head count so that you can negotiate the price of the shirts based on volume. Generally, when you are ordering by volume, the more you order, the more you can negotiate the price. Knowing the details of your attendance gives you an advantage when negotiating—not only can you lower the price, it also tells the supplier that you are organized and capable.

How do you determine how many people will attend the reunion? First, try to get an idea of the full scope of your family. Then, take a poll. Find out how many would be interested in attending a family reunion. If you have a small family, you can usually find out the answers to both of these questions at the same time. If you have a large family, it may take several separate efforts on your part to get the information that you need.

GETTING INFORMATION

To begin estimating all of the potential attendees to the reunion, start by compiling a list of the entire family. The quickest way to start collecting names is to telephone the relative who has the most knowledge about the family. When I want to know something about my family, I usually start with my mother, who then calls my grandmother. We can all talk at the same time using the three-way calling service provided by our local telephone company. Three-way calling is a convenient method of contacting multiple family members simultaneously. This service is also called conference calling. With three-way calling, there is usually a per-use fee, so use it sparingly.

Once your family members start reminiscing, they may recall branches of relations you never knew you had. Some of the most fascinating and spontaneous stories can come from prodding the memories of your relatives. Hearing the sounds of their voices, listening to their stories, can really put you in a nostalgic mood—and in for a long conversation. That's when you have to be the most careful.

One downside to using the telephone to collect your information is the cost. If the knowledgeable relative lives out of state or even out of the country, long-distance charges could put a damper on the conversation. Yet, the memories of your family members are too precious to have to cut short. Also, you don't want to hurt anyone's feelings by interrupting in the middle of a reverie.

If it's just the straight facts that you're looking for, consider creating a form letter or questionnaire. Mail it out to the relatives you would have contacted by telephone. This will give your relatives all the time they need to reminisce about the *old times* and about how your third cousin so-and-so did such-and-such. Also, the longer the family members who are recalling the names have to think and recall the family tree, the less likely that some branch will be left off the list.

To supplement the memories of your relatives, scour every available source for information. Other sources of information about your family include old letters, photographs, and home movies. Get your family members to hunt through their attics and basements, hope chests, storage areas, and family Bibles for clues to the branches of your family tree. For extensive searches, go to the library for town phone directories or genealogy information.

It doesn't matter if your family is big or small, lives in one region, or is scattered across the world, it's going to take time to contact most representatives of your family tree. Give yourself plenty of time to collect the names.

For example, my maternal side of the family is very large. My grandmother had eleven surviving children. Each aunt, uncle, and cousin is a potential reunion attendee. However you won't know the full amount of relatives to attend the reunion until you start to collect the names.

Attempting to list each potential attendee of the reunion, I start off with a rough list of my aunts and uncles. Under each name, I list their children. And, if applicable, I list their children's children.

GETTING INFORMATION BACK

Getting a full list of names in a timely manner is key to planning your reunion. Keep in mind your family's busy schedules. They may put off filling out the questionnaire until the last minute. Sometimes, papers get lost. Be prepared to mail the questionnaire a couple of times. Make the information-gathering process as effortless as possible for all parties involved. Make sure you clearly state on the form when you need the information. You may even want to send a reminder notice or call a week in advance of your due date.

If you provide several options for returning the questionnaire, you'll increase your chances of getting information back quickly. It might be helpful, for example, to include a self-addressed stamped envelope. Or, if you have a home computer with a fax modem or access to a fax machine, allow family members to send information that way. Even if your relatives do not have access to this type of equipment in their own homes, fax machines are available in many places where they are likely to go—such as banks, libraries, grocery stores, and post offices.

In the age of the information superhighway, using the World Wide Web and e-mail to contact your relatives is another way to collect facts.

You could use any one of these options—or a combination—to compile the list of family names. Do what makes the most sense for the amount of time that you have to plan and your budget. The point is to get the most accurate information in the quickest amount of time.

Offer an incentive to getting the material back on time such as a discount on T-shirt prices. And always, always follow up with a thank-you note or phone call once you do receive your information. Everyone wants to feel appreciated and it will guarantee a good start to the event.

If you have a large family and you're planning by committee, consider having multiple researchers. You can designate several family members to research each branch of the family.

Organizing the Information

How you keep this list of names isn't as important as making the list as complete as possible. You may decide to keep all of the names and addresses in a notebook or on index cards. Or, advises Orlean Dorsey, "Take advantage of technology, such as computers. There are many software packages perfect for building databases of family members."

To help keep all of the information you uncover organized and under control, keep the names listed alphabetically. Keeping your research in a loose-leaf binder or in a computer file will make the information easy to update. You can add to the list easily. Also keeping it up to date will help the organizers of future events—whether it's you or if you've passed the mantle on to someone else.

When you compile the list of names, make sure to keep track of information such as:

- Full names

- Addresses

- Phone numbers

- The person's relationship to you, such as your cousin or great-aunt

- Something personal, an achievement worth noting, such as being the first to graduate from college

- Family members' special interests or abilities. Keeping track of special interests and abilities may come in very handy when looking for volunteers to help you coordinate events for the family reunion

- Occupation since some relatives may be able to donate services or ask for contributions from their employer

* * * * *

ESTIMATE THE ATTENDANCE

You've done a lot of legwork by tracking down individual family members. Now that you have the names and addresses of your relatives, use a combination of contacting them by phone, mailings, and e-mail to get a good feel for how many of your relatives would be interested in getting together for a reunion. If you have a small family, you may be able to get their personal information and their preferences done with one round of phone calls or one mailing.

If your family is large or widely scattered, phone calls are unwieldy. However, a family reunion survey does involve contacting all. Your survey will give you an idea of how to focus the reunion. In your survey, make sure to include questions covering the following:

- The number of people in the immediate family—this question is a good cross check against the information you gathered while you were researching family names

- Their addresses, telephone and fax numbers, and e-mail addresses

- Whether they are interested in attending a family reunion

- How many people are expected to attend from that family

- When and where the reunion should be held

- Interest in volunteering to provide reunion support

- Length of the reunion

- Family reunion theme

- What music or entertainment would they enjoy

SAMPLE SURVEY

The tone of the survey should be warm and friendly. It should let your relatives know how important they are to the success of the family reunion. For the survey, the more questions you include, the easier it will be to plan the details of the reunion. The following provides an example of a letter to help you gather some information.

CALLING ALL FAMILY MEMBERS!!!

How long has it been since . . .
You've seen Uncle Joe?
You've had a tantalizing taste of
Grandma's sweet potato pie?
You've held the latest addition to the family?

Did you know you even had *an Uncle Joe?*
Well, maybe it's time you did!

We're looking for all members of the family to
take part in our first annual family reunion.
If you're interested in having, hosting, or helping out
at our reunion, fill out these few easy questions
and send them back in the envelope provided.

Remember, you are an important part of this family!
The sooner we get your information,
the better our family reunion will be.
Please return the survey by February 1.
Thank you!

REUNION SURVEY

Family Information:

Number of members in your immediate family: _____

List their names and ages: _____

_____

What is your current address? Street _____

City_____State_____Zip_____

Telephone _____ Fax _____ E-mail _____

(If any family members are living on their own, please provide above information for them as well.)

Reunion Information:

Would you be interest in attending a family reunion?
_____

Where should the reunion be held?
_____

Would you be willing to travel to another city/state to attend a family reunion?
_____

How much would you be willing to pay to attend?
_____

How many people are expected to attend from your family?
_____

When is a good time to hold the reunion?
_____

How long should the reunion last? A day? A weekend? A week?
_____

Suggest some possible themes for the family reunion.
_____

What music or entertainment would you enjoy?
_____

Do you play an instrument? Would you like to perform at the reunion?
_____

Would you be interested in volunteering to provide reunion support?
_____

Would you be interested in bringing a dish to the reunion? Entrée, Side dish? Dessert? List your specialty.
_____

Please answer these questions and return in the envelope provided. If you have any questions, contact the reunion coordinator.

Be sure to include the contact name and information on the survey itself. Each respondent may have a different opinion when and where the reunion should be held. Don't get discouraged. As you sift through the responses, you will discover a pattern. Maybe most of the responses will show a specific season, such as the springtime or Christmas, if not a specific month or day. Or maybe several of the responses will show a preference for a sentimental location, such as the family homestead or the birthplace of the oldest family member. Make sure to be diligent and log the dates, places, and number of people.

REMEMBRANCES OF REUNIONS PAST:
ORLEAN DORSEY, JACKSON FAMILY REUNION

I estimate the size of my family reunions based on polls from previous reunions. It never fails, however, that no matter how close you think you can hit the mark, there are either more or less people than you anticipated. One year, we held a reunion where almost everything was free. We had between 250 and 300 people show up. The next year, we tried to recoup some costs by charging for some things. People knew up front that they had to pay. The turnout wasn't quite as big then. The trick is to come up with a balance between getting people to come to the reunion and not putting all the cost on the same people.

When you have more people than you expect show up, the biggest problem is figuring out if you've got enough food. You want to make sure that everyone gets enough to eat. One year, we handed out tickets in order for family members to get their meals. For the most part, it worked pretty well. But that plan had its share of problems. Whether it was true or not, people claimed that they had lost their tickets. What are you supposed to do? You can't turn them away. And there are those who you know, through some kind of hook up, are going to get more than one ticket. But you can't prove that someone has been through the food line more than one time. You're stuck with the same problem. The complaint that some people didn't get a chance to eat was enough to make me want to think of a different solution.

One year, I thought I'd get smart. I wanted to eliminate the problem of the lost or multiple tickets. I contacted a medical-supply company and ordered some wristbands. You know the kind—the ones that they put on you when you're in the hospital. It's almost impossible to lose those. I placed them in the packets family members received when they registered for the reunion. It cut down on the lost-ticket complaint. As long as they kept their wristband, they could eat as much as they wanted.

5

DEFINING THE DETAILS

What happens to a dream deferred?
—"DREAM DEFERRED" BY LANGSTON HUGHES

Y ou've taken the first steps toward planning your
family reunion. You've tracked down branches of
your family. Also you've surveyed them to get an idea of the
best time and place to host the reunion. The ideas are pour-
ing in. Each idea may seem better than the last. Because
there are so many good ideas, it may be difficult to narrow
down your choices.

Or, maybe you've experienced just the opposite response.
Perhaps the responses to your survey have been lukewarm,
giving you little direction on how to proceed. If you don't
receive responses to your survey questions, you have one of
three options on how to proceed.

First, you can wait a little longer to see if more surveys
come in. However, if you wait too long, you may have to
settle for a less elaborate reunion than you originally
intended to host. The more time you wait, the less time you
have to plan. Planning makes the difference between a
reunion that goes smoothly and one that appears as if it was
haphazardly thrown together. Though, there's something to
be said for spontaneity, well-organized reunions have far

less stress and confusion for those hosting the event and the attending relatives. There will be no milling around wondering what to do next and no wondering who is in charge of what.

Your second option is to resend the reunion surveys with increased pleas for responses. However, this will incur extra printing and postage costs which will eat into your budget. When you send out your surveys the first time, you can expect for some of your relatives to lose them. The cost of resending a handful of surveys will not greatly affect your budget; however resending *all* surveys with the hope of getting a response does have a negative effect. Money that is spent trying to gather information is money that could have been applied elsewhere.

If you are not getting responses from your surveys, your third option is to place the idea of the reunion on hold until you generate more interest. You know when your family loses interest in your reunion when attendance drops dramatically. Or, you will see the same faces over and over.

Whether the responses to your surveys have been overwhelming or overly apathetic, you must make a decision to have enough time to turn plans and ideas into action. If it has been a while since your family has gotten together, your decision may be easier; chances are that they feel the same need for connection that you have.

TIPS FOR THE SINGLE-PERSON ORGANIZER

If you are the single-person organizer, you will be defining most of the details. Your vision of how the reunion should be run sets the pace and tone. Your energy and creativity will reflect itself in the events and activities. However, as the reunion organizer, you must also listen to the voices of your relatives. By returning the surveys, your relatives have given their vote and their voice toward defining reunion details. Just as a politician must heed the voice of the constituents, you must listen to the voice of your relatives. As an example, if the reunion surveys you get back indicate that your relatives support a summer reunion, a reunion planned in the dead of winter would probably have a very low attendance. If you are too far off the mark from your relatives' suggested dates and times, you may find yourself voted out of office at the next reunion with someone else at the head of the planning.

TIPS FOR COMMITTEE PLANNERS

When planning by committee, determining the details of the reunion can be a lot of fun. Something happens when a group of enthusiastic, creative people with a common goal comes together. Once the ideas start flowing, you will be surprised how one idea builds on the next. And the next. And the next. You may start off considering a one-day picnic, but end up planning a weeklong cruise. If this is your first time planning a family reunion, it's best to keep the reunion simple. After you have a few successful reunions under your belt, you can work toward more elaborate ones.

Because there are so many good ideas that can come out of the planning committee, it may be difficult to choose from the best one. Try to come to a consensus, one in which everyone commits to the idea. List the ideas and vote on each one. Use either a show of hands or a secret ballot. How you vote isn't as important as making sure that everyone agrees on the best way to proceed.

Once you come up with a plan, stick to it. The more you make changes, the more confusion. The more confusion, the harder it will be to carry out your plan.

What Type of Reunion Should You Have?

Deciding the kind of reunion to have depends on how long you want it to last. Should it be a one-day event? Should it last an entire weekend? Should the reunion cover a week? The reunion surveys that you mailed to your relatives will give you an idea of the length of the reunion. However, if this is your first time planning a family reunion, keep it simple. One-day events, such as a family picnic, are the easiest to plan.

One-Day Event

One-day reunions work well with families who live close together, either in the same state or nearby. Picnics are popular choices for one-day reunions because they are informal. Family members can kick back, relax, and mingle with their relatives at their own pace. Or, they can get revved up and participate in the planned activities. If you decide on a picnic, choose a location big enough to accommodate your family. If your family is large, wide-open spaces provided by parks and recreational facilities (such as forest preserves, reservoirs, lakes, and beaches) are popular locations. If your family reunion will be small to medium-size (from fifty to one-hundred and fifty members), family property is also an option for hosting your family reunion picnic.

Multiday events

How do you know if your family would enjoy a reunion that lasts for several days? If the surveys indicate your family would be willing to pay a little extra and travel a little farther for the benefit of extended company, that's one indication that you could plan for a longer reunion. Reunions that last several days are usually planned to coincide with a weekend or a holiday.

Selecting a Site for a One-Day Event

Where will the reunion be held? The person or committee hosting the reunion will usually plan it for an area that's most convenient for them to manage. Trying to coordinate a location out of the state can be tricky. Not impossible—just tricky.

When you send out your survey and you want to make certain that the reunion is held in your own state, be clear in your cover letter that the location has already been selected.

However, if the location is open, and the site of choice is not in the area of the planners, you will have to rely on the relatives living nearest to the site to make certain the planned events are well-coordinated and carried out. Keep in mind, however, that reunions that are hosted outside of the planner's area have higher telephone bills and greater travel expenses.

Sometimes, it makes sense for the reunion to be held in a location away from those planning the reunion. Mary Livingston lives in Houston, Texas. Yet, for several years, the family reunion was held in LaGrange, Texas. LaGrange is the site of the original Jackson homestead. It seemed natural to want to go "back home" and to call all of their relatives there again. When planning their family reunion, Mrs. Livingston relied on her cousin who lived on the homestead to prepare the site for the family reunion. As the reunion time drew near, Mrs. Livingston traveled to the homestead site several times to help arrange for the hotel, food, decorations, and so on.

If you plan to hold the reunion away from your home, make sure to include expenses for travel to and from the site in your budget. These expenses will include gas, food, hotel room, and airline tickets. Remember, an out-of-state site may not be cost effective for a one-day event.

Once you have an idea of how many will attend the reunion and where it will be, you can figure out where to put everyone during the duration of the reunion.

- Hotel/Motel chains: take advantage of discount group rates offered by chains.

- Family home: opening up your home to your relatives may foster a feeling of togetherness if your family reunion is small and manageable.

- Bed-and-breakfast inns: caters to small family reunions with a cozy atmosphere and intimate surroundings.

REMEMBRANCES OF REUNIONS PAST:
KRYSTAL WILLIAMS ON THE JACKSON FAMILY REUNION, 1992

For many years, the Jackson Family Reunion has been held at the family homestead site established in the late 1800's in LaGrange, Texas. The entire place has a feel of the Old West to it, with fenced-in pastures penning in the family's horses and even a few cows. Old wagon wheels mark the entrance to the gate leading up to the main house. For the 1992 family reunion, the Jackson Family planned trail rides and hayrides to add to the flavor of the western frontier.

REMEMBRANCES OF REUNIONS PAST:
VALERIE MERLETT, SIMMONS FAMILY REUNION, 1997

One year, we had our family reunion at my aunt's house. When I was a little girl, I always shared a room with my cousin. I came to think of that room as my room, too. When it was time for the family reunion, the first thing I did was take my bags up to *my* room. By this time, my cousin had moved away. She'd also gotten married. Yet, she still considered that room to be hers, too.

When I looked over and saw a strange person's bags in *our* room, I said, "Oh, no. Whoever that is is just going to have to find another place to sleep tonight. This is our room."

It turned out to be her husband's luggage. But did that matter? Of course not! This was my room, my bed. He had to pick up all of his bags and find another place to sleep. I think he wound up sleeping with the kids.

Weekend Reunion

Selecting a Location for a Weekend Event

For a weekend reunion, the location is equally important. Since the family will be spending more time together, a site that is easily accessible, safe, and comfortable is key to having a successful reunion. Hotels or motels are the most convenient choices.

Selecting a Hotel

You should start researching hotels no later than six months before the reunion. Your budget will be a heavy deciding factor on which hotel to select. How much are family members willing to pay? Your survey will give you an idea of the price range. If you opt for a cheaper hotel rate, you may save a few dollars, but may sacrifice quality of service and accommodations. Higher priced hotels offer more amenities, but the cost of the rooms may be out of range for your family members. Search for hotels in the mid-price range in your city. The higher-priced hotels are usually located near business districts or popular tourists attractions. Lower-priced hotels are usually in suburban areas or small towns.

Negotiate a Contract with the Hotel

Once you decide on a location and a hotel, establish a contract with the hotel. A mutually agreed upon contract will detail what the hotel is responsible for providing, at what prices, as well as what you will be responsible for. When you negotiate with the hotel, be very specific about what you will need. Take a checklist with you. The checklist should include the number of rooms you will need to book, whether you need a banquet hall, and so on. As with any situation, both parties will want to get the best deal.

Reserving Rooms

Many organizers book a block of rooms for family members attending the reunion. Family members can then make their own reservations. As a bargaining point, you may want to try to get the hotel to waive cancellation fees if family members are not able to honor the reservations. Try to avoid collecting money for the hotel rooms. You will save time, effort, money, and frustration if you are not responsible for collecting money for the individual rooms. Even when you announce deadlines and notify family members well in advance, there will be family members who do not come up with the necessary funds to rent a hotel room until the week of the reunion. If you are trying to reserve a block of rooms in advance, last-minute payers can put a crimp in your plans. It will save time and residual ill will if individual family members are responsible for paying for their own rooms.

If you do have to collect money to make the hotel reservations, make sure that family members know when you absolutely must have the money. Tell them that any monies delivered after that point, will not guarantee them a room. Communicate the deadlines as often as possible. But when it comes down to the deadline and monies are not received, be gracious but remain firm.

6

FINANCING THE REUNION

Your wealth can be stolen,
but precious riches buried deep in your soul cannot.
—MINNIE RIPERTON

The magic, the moments, and the memories created by your family reunion are priceless. Seeing a loved one you haven't seen in years or holding your newborn baby relative in your arms for the first time—those are memories you cannot put a price on.

Unfortunately, coordinating the series of events leading up to those moments do have inherent costs. Keep in mind the telephone calls and the mailings to entice your family members to the reunion, the food your relatives will eat, the hotel rooms they will occupy, the keepsakes and mementos they will take back with them—all of the elements have a price tag associated with them.

To make sure that the price tag doesn't become a hindrance to getting your relatives together, follow some of the suggested guidelines below to come up with a sound financial plan.

Set a Budget

A budget is a record of how much money you have to spend and how you're going to spend it. When you create your budget, try to be as specific as possible as you list all of the items and activities that are going to cost you money. It helps to keep track of the costs if you think of the reunion expenses in stages.

Before-Reunion Expenses

Before-reunion expenses include all of the costs you will incur while preparing for the reunion. Examples of these expenses include:

- Awards or recognition for all of the volunteers, planners, and contributors to the reunion
- Banking fees, such as for checking accounts
- Decorations, such as banners and signs
- Deposits for hotels, photographers, musicians
- Keepsakes such as T-shirts, hats, and memory books
- Park permits
- Photocopying for printing flyers and newsletters
- Picnic foods and supplies
- Postage, envelopes, and related costs to mailings
- Telephone calls

During-Reunion Expenses

These are expenses that will have to be paid while the reunion is going on. Some examples of these costs include:

- Disc jockey or musicians
- Fresh foods or beverages
- Generators to supply power for the deejay or additional lights
- Guest speaker
- Photographer
- Portable toilet
- Tents (pavillion-style and play tents for the kids)

After-Reunion Expenses

After your reunion is over, there are usually miscellaneous bills and expenses that must be cleared. Paying these expenses promptly and in full generates goodwill between you and the parties involved. Building a good relationship while planning the reunion can only increase your bargaining power when it comes to planning and negotiating prices for the next reunion. Some examples of after-the-reunion expenses include:

- Hotel bill
- Reunion site clean up detail
- Postage and stationery for additional reunion information

A budget gives you a rough idea of estimated expenses. Remember, you may not come up with every possible cost. Even experienced reunion planners can't think of every contingency. However, the more detailed you are with how much money you think you will spend, the easier it will be to plan the fund-raisers and request the dues to pay for your reunion.

There are two methods I find useful when trying to come up with budget lists. The sit-and-stew method and brainstorming.

Sit-and-Stew Method

Your brain is a powerful ally. It can work on a problem even after you think you've put the problem out of your mind. The sit-and-stew method of problem solving lets your mind's creative power take over while you move on to other tasks.

As a single-person organizer, there is a lot of pressure on you to "get it right." When it comes to financial matters, there isn't much room for mistakes. Either you have enough money or you don't. You want to be as complete as possible when planning your budget to avoid any shortfalls. The goal is to have enough money left over to begin planning for the next reunion.

After you create a first-pass list of possible expenses as described in the pre-, during-, and after-reunion expenses sections, set the list aside for a while—an hour, a day, or a couple of days. The pressure of trying to cover every possibility may cramp your creative style while you're staring at the blank page. Put down the ideas that come to you right off, then concentrate on another planning activity phase for a while. When you least expect it, another idea will pop into your head. Add that idea to your list and keep going. At the end of the stewing period, your list should be more indicative of the costs you can expect to incur.

Brainstorming

Another method of trying to come up with multiple ideas is through brainstorming. Brainstorming is considering or investigating (an issue, for example) by engaging in shared problem solving. Brainstorming works well with committees.

When the budget or finance committee meets to discuss funding the reunion, let someone throw out an idea. Another person then adds to the idea. And another person does the same. Keep building on the list.

In a brainstorming session, accept all ideas, big and small. Some ideas may sound perfect to you. Some may sound ridiculous. Resist the temptation to ridicule those unlikely sounding ideas. Keep the sessions upbeat and lively. This will encourage the planning committee to be free about their ideas. If the committee shoots down any idea, you may prevent the *one* idea you needed from surfacing.

REFINING THE BUDGET

After you have made a first pass at the potential reunion activities, fill in the list with the items that support those activities. Think in terms of what you want, how many, and at what cost. Trying to figure out cost is the budget-estimation phase.

For example, if you plan to have a one-day picnic, and you want to have games at that picnic, make a list of all of the games that you want to include. Suppose you want to play volleyball at your reunion. What items will you need to purchase in order to support this activity? How many nets? How many balls? What do these items cost? Even if some family members volunteer to donate or loan these items to you, what is the cost of replacing them if they are damaged or lost?

ESTIMATING COSTS

Suppose you want to purchase three volleyball sets. If each set costs around twenty-five dollars, you can estimate the total cost like this:

3 (number of sets) × $25 (cost of set) = $75.

Don't forget to include any applicable sales tax in your estimates.

Estimating the costs of your reunion is only part of the process of refining your budget. If you feel comfortable with those estimates, base your bottom line for fund-raising on them. Again, the goal is to get as close as possible to the actual cost of the reunion. You can refine your estimated costs by doing a little legwork. Go out to local shops and stores and do actual pricing to see how close you came to the mark.

Sometimes, when you go out to get actual pricing, you still may have to adjust your calculations. Sometimes you may have to pad your figures. Padding means adding a little extra to cover possible changes in price.

For example, you are on the food committee and wish to know how much to allow for purchasing twenty loaves of bread. The week you investigate, bread is listed at $1 per loaf. Twenty loaves of bread will cost twenty dollars. However, on the week you go to purchase the bread, perhaps the price has risen to $1.05 per loaf. Now the cost is twenty-one dollars. A one dollar difference may not seem like much now, but consistently, over the course of your reunion planning, shortfalls do add up.

When making a budget, the only time you should not have to pad it is when you have a written contract spelling out exactly how much a good or service will cost. For example, suppose you want a disc jockey to play music at your reunion. What does that deejay charge per hour? Multiply that cost by the number of hours you want the deejay to perform. That fee will not change. However, if the deejay is really good, and people are into the music, you may want the deejay to stay a little longer. Build that contingency into your budget.

If you are an experienced family reunion planner, setting up a budget may not require as much legwork. You have enough experience to be able to guesstimate how much something will cost. If the last five reunions wound up costing between $3000 and $4000, and this reunion will be very similar, you can base your fundraising needs on that amount. However, being a good guesser is no substitute for having the facts to back you up.

CREATE A REUNION BANK ACCOUNT

A special account for all of the funds generated for and by the family reunion is a good idea. These funds should be separate from your personal funds. It's up to you whether you'd want to transfer any of your *personal* funds into the family reunion account. If you do, just remember that you are doing so freely, out of the goodness of your heart, and in the spirit of the family reunion.

If you donate personal funds to help offset reunion costs, and you are planning by committee, the occasion may arise when you disagree with how the funds should be allocated. Don't use your *gift* as a means of bending the other committee members to your will. Remember that everyone is contributing something to the reunion and every contribution is valuable.

Deciding when and how the money is taken from the reunion account may go smoother if you set up your account with a double-signature safeguard. That way, no money can be removed from the account unless two authorized parties sign a check.

RAISING FUNDS

Once you establish your budget, you can begin to raise money to cover reunion costs. To cover the before-reunion costs, start with a request for seed money. Seed money is money given to the reunion effort to get it off the ground.

You can start by asking the members of the committee for a small donation. Depending on the size of the committee, a donation of $5 to $10 a person can cover some initial costs, such as paper and postage for your initial communications with your family.

Other Fundraising Ideas

Each family, whether located locally or spread out, can participate with fundraising events. When several families are located locally, they can combine their efforts. If families are scattered, they can hold individual fundraisers.

One way to generate interest and money for the reunion is to have a fundraising contest. The family that generates the most money for the reunion wins a prize, such as a free night at the hotel.

Some fundraising ideas include:

- Car wash. Contact local, popular fast-food restaurant or grocery store to use their parking lot. Use the seed money collected by the reunion committee to purchase items such as signs to advertise the car wash, buckets, sponges, hoses, soap, and drying towels, or these can be donated by family members.

- Bake sale. If you have family members who love to cook, ask them to volunteer to provide items such as cookies, cakes, pies, and so on. Seed money can be used to purchase baking ingredients such as flour, eggs, sugar, and baking pans. Try to get family members to donate their time and resources in order to reserve the seed money for other reunion expenses.

- Skating party. Contact a local skating rink and negotiate the price for the skating rink. You will get a better negotiated price if you pick a nonpeak night.

- Auction or a garage sale. Ask your family members to supply items such as clothing, furniture, books, or toys.

- Raffle tickets. Prizes can be donated from family members, local businesses, or purchased from seed money.

Family Dues

Another way to generate money is to request money from family members who will be attending the reunion. Dues or registration fees will cover the bulk of the reunion costs. As an incentive to ensure all family members attend, offer special, reduced fees for children and senior citizens who might be on a fixed income instead of a flat fee.

Tourism Bureaus

Tourism Bureaus and Chambers of Commerce cannot donate funds to your reunion, but they are an excellent source of freebies. Coupons to local attractions, souvenirs, and tourist-attraction pamphlets can help offset some of the costs of trying to entertain your family members every moment. A list of state bureaus is located in an appendix in the back of this planning guide.

KEEPING TRACK OF EXPENSES

When it comes to figuring out ways to raise money for your family reunion, use your imagination. Be creative. However, when it comes to keeping track of *how* much money you have to spend, it's better if you're not so creative. Use tried-and-true methods to keep track of reunion expenses. If you have a time-honored system in place, it's easier to find mistakes if they ever arise.

Keeping track of how, when, and where reunion money is spent is crucial. Only in that way can you be certain that you do not run out of money before the reunion is over. The goal of the reunion is to have fun and maybe turn a little profit to be applied to the next reunion.

If your family is large and you expect to generate a lot of funds, consider hiring an accountant to track your expenses for you. Remember to include the accountant's fees within your budget.

Another way to keep track of your expenses is with a computer. Software programs such as Quicken or Microsoft Money will help you manage your money. These programs sometimes come already installed on your computer. If they are not, they can be purchased for a reasonable fee. Both programs generate easy-to-read reports that will help make sense of all of the debits and credits to your family reunion account.

If you don't have access to a computer, another method of keeping track of expenses is through the old-fashioned ledger book. Ledger books are available at your local office-supply store, or through general-merchandise stores such as Wal-Mart or Target. Writing your expenses in a ledger book provides a portable record of your money-management efforts.

Even though an entire committee may manage the family reunion funds, it is usually best if one person is responsible for maintaining the ledger book. This person will be coordinator of all the bills, receipts, and influxes of cash that must be recorded in the ledger. If the ledger book is not passed from committee to committee or family to family, there is less chance for errors.

SAMPLE BUDGET

The following provides an example of some careful record keeping. This budget comes from Orlean Dorsey for the

1994 Jackson family reunion. The items enclosed in paren-
theses indicate a surplus or small profit.

JACKSON FAMILY REUNION
1994 Budget

Description	Budgeted Amount	Actual Amount	Difference
Before-Reunion Costs			
Administrative Cost	$50.00	$50.00	$0.00
Banquet Room (deposit)	75.00	50.00	(25.00)
Decorations	75.00	0.00	(75.00)
Ice and Ice-Box Rental	75.00	75.00	0.00
Trophies and Plaques	50.00	59.54	9.54
T-shirt Order	500.00	769.98	269.98
During-Reunion Costs			
Cleanup for Picnic Area	400.00	515.00	115.00
Food—Banquet	500.00	500.00	0.00
Food—Picnic	400.00	400.00	0.00
Food—Sunday Breakfast	0.00	85.00	85.00
Fresh Fruit	40.00	0.00	(40.00)
Miscellaneous	130.00	403.85	273.85
Moon Walk	200.00	200.00	0.00
Party Rentals	75.00	37.87	(37.13)
Pool Party	100.00	0.00	(100.00)
Portable Toilet	80.00	81.19	1.19
Program Printing	50.00	19.53	(30.47)
Tent Rental	0.00	20.00	20.00
After-Reunion Costs			
Utilities (Water and Electricity)	200.00	210.00	10.00
Totals	$3,000.00	$3,476.96	$476.96

REMEMBRANCES OF REUNIONS PAST:
ORLEAN L. DORSEY, JACKSON FAMILY REUNION, JULY 1997

Our family has been very blessed in recent years. We have
not had many deaths. However, this past reunion was orga-

nized by other relatives, which gave me an opportunity to sit alone and reflect on three very dear relatives that have passed away. The first time I decided to organize our family reunion was shortly after my uncle Fred Jenkins had shared something very personal with me. He was terminally ill and was very upset at how some of our relatives and friends took life for granted.

Fred was very helpful because he had organized a couple of class reunions. His best advice to me was "give it up while you still can." He warned me that there would be times when I'd be very discouraged because no matter how much I planned, people wouldn't respond and it would seem as if they didn't care. He was right. I didn't get much response until the very day of the reunion. I had gone over-budget and only a fraction of the people who said they would participate had actually paid. However, I was very proud of the fact that my family showed up in the end and everyone had a great time.

My sister Anita Dorsey-Cain, and my aunt Suandra Jackson both passed away unexpectedly. Suandra died shortly after the '96 reunion and Anita died just before the '98 reunion. Both were godly women and both sure could cook. It was Fred's dream to keep the family together and it was Anita and Suandra's deaths that reminded me of what family reunions are all about. No longer will I be a stick in the mud, worrying about recovering the money I put in. If I end up financing future reunions with 100 percent of my own money, it will be money well spent as long as people show up.

7

SPREADING THE WORD

As soon as healing takes place, go out and heal somebody else.

—MAYA ANGELOU

Though some of the finer details of your reunion may not be sorted out until the last few weeks, don't let communicating the family reunion be a last-minute detail. If you are a single-person organizer, this is the moment when you should act as the town crier—making sure that everyone knows of your family reunion plans. If you are planning your reunion by committee, the correspondence committee is responsible for making sure the details of the family reunion reach each and every family member. You'll have a higher attendance rate if your family members can plan to attend. Also, giving enough notice means that your family members will have enough time to make travel plans or request vacation time.

By this time, you've already generated your family's interest and enthusiasm by sending out the surveys. Keep up the interest by giving regular updates on the reunion. For example, if you begin planning the reunion six months to a year in advance of the event (and a year is a long time to remain enthusiastic about anything), you may want to send a notice announcing the tentative plans for your family reunion. Again, all of the fine details need not be set, but the early notices should give enough details to help your family members plan for the reunion. Keep the early notices brief, but enticing. Provide a tantalizing bit of information that will grab and hold their interest in the interim.

You should plan on keeping in touch with your family at least three times during the planning phases. Many families use a combination of methods to communicate with their family—from simple postcards to elaborate web pages.

NOTE CARDS/POSTCARDS

Note cards and postcards are inexpensive to purchase and to mail. However, they do not leave much room to place detailed information. To keep down costs, use notecards and postcards to give the preliminary details of the family reunion. These type of cards are good for preliminary notices and follow-up reminder notices.

One drawback to using postcards, however, is getting the information on the cards. You can send the information written by hand for that personal touch. However, if you have an extensive family, just getting the notices written and mailed can be time-consuming. One solution is to have a local print shop print the messages you want on the post-card. Remember, however, the money you save by using postcards will be taken up with printing costs.

Or, you can purchase sheets of perforated or pre-cut paper from an office-supply store. You can save time by using a computer to create a standard message and printing the notices on the card-stock paper. Then, simply "punch" out the individual cards, apply your mailing label and postage, and mail.

FLYERS

A flyer is a single sheet of paper designed to provide information while catching one's eye. For other correspondences with your family, send out the flyers that describe in detail what to expect from the family reunion. These flyers may include all of the information the family needs to attend the reunion, such as dates and times of events, deadline information (such as for hotel registrations), any dues or fees, special themes, and what items, if any, should be brought to the reunion.

Again, to save costs, flyers can be printed on plain paper. Or you can make the flyer more festive to generate interest by printing on brightly colored paper. Bright colors such as yellow or pink may look attractive, but they also cost a little more.

REMINDERS

Reminders give all of the last-minute details that solidify the family reunicn and gently prompt anyone who has not paid his or her dues or registration fees to get those checks or money orders in. To soften the blow of having to remind your relatives to pay their fees, include a warm and sincere note indicating how much you're looking forward to seeing them all.

Sample—Early Notice

This sample notice, courtesy of Mary Livingston (Jackson Family Reunion, June 1997) was mailed as a simple flyer.

Greetings to every member of the Jackson Family.
This year the location of the reunion
has moved to the Dallas area.
Our host and hostess will be Pat and Louis Gonzales.
Reunion events will include
a Get-Acquainted Fish Fry, Barbecue with all the fixin's,
games and contests, family history, and quilt signing.
Dates for the reunion are June 26 through June 28.

Newsletters

If it has been a long time since your family has gotten together, there may be a lot of information that cannot be covered in a single flyer. One way to spread information throughout the family is through a family newsletter. With a newsletter, you have more space and the freedom to be creative. With all of the possible computer software packages, clip art, and scanning techniques (getting pictures or text into a computer file you can change on the screen) on the market, you have the ability to create a document that captures the spirit of your family reunion. You may need an entire committee just to maintain the newsletter alone. Newsletters can be typed, created by you on a computer, or professionally done by a graphic designer. Here are some guidelines for creating a newsletter that will suit your needs.

Gather Samples

When in doubt, look to other sources for ideas. If you're not sure how to start a newsletter, begin by gathering samples. Look for the samples that catch your eye and hold your interest such as the weekly circulars that are often stuffed into your mailbox. Don't just automatically throw those away. Review them for ideas on how to present certain types of information. Circulars like these make it a point to present the best way of asking for money. You could take a hint or two from them when it comes time to ask for registration fees or family dues. Church bulletins and announcements, single-page grocery store flyers, even lost dog posters—all of these have elements you can borrow from to help you plan your newsletter.

If you have just a few pieces of information you want to pass along, a simple two-page newsletter may do the trick.

If you have to catch the family up on a lot of information, a four- or eight-page newsletter may be more appropriate. How often you decide to publish the newsletter depends on three main elements: how much information you have to share, how much time you can devote to creating the newsletter, and the budget.

Though the ideas and information that will go into the newsletter come from several sources, the task of putting the newsletter together usually falls to one person—the editor. The editor is responsible for reviewing all of the stories, selecting the ones that will go into the newsletter, and ultimately making certain that the newsletter is printed and mailed. If you are that person, putting the newsletter out on a regular basis is essential to generating interest. Family members eagerly look forward to seeing their name in print. One way to keep a regular schedule is to follow one of these patterns:

● Annually—Newsletters are mailed out once a year. The multiple-page newsletter usually fits well into this schedule because so much can happen in the span of a year.

● Biannually—Newsletters are mailed out twice a year.

● Tri-annually—Newsletters are mailed out every four months.

● Quarterly—Newsletters are mailed out four times a year.

How often newsletters are mailed out is often determined by the budget. Making copies of the newsletter can become costly. Even if you decide to print out all of the copies from the computer, you have the extra cost of paper and the wear and tear on your toner cartridge (laser printers) or ink cartridges (ink-jet printers).

Creating a Newsletter

The best way to create a newsletter is on a computer. That way you can make changes quickly so you don't have to have the entire newsletter completed and printed before you get an idea of how it will look.

Word-processing software has become very sophisticated within the past decade. Old-style word-processing software such as WordPerfect or Word Star would not let you "see" how your design looked without printing out the page first. If you're experimenting with your newsletter, making mistakes can be costly in time, money, and resources. Many word-processing software programs now include a design element called WYSIWYG (What You See Is What You Get). When you type information on a page and include graphics (pictures, clip art, or stylized text), what you see on the screen is what will print on the page.

The word-processing software on your computer may also incorporate templates. A template is a pattern or guide to follow when designing the newsletter. Newsletter templates show you how to arrange information in one or more columns. Templates also give you an idea of the best place to include pictures and, if your budget permits, color. Templates give you a starting point for helping you to develop your own style.

If you're not comfortable using a computer, don't let that be a hindrance to getting information out to your family. Copy centers such as Kwik Kopy or Kinko's have employees who will help you design your newsletter for a fee. They usually charge by the hour. However, the more complex your newsletter, the higher the cost. If you provide the text, pictures, clip art, and an "idea" how you want the newsletter to look, they will create a design for you.

For a successful, professional-looking newsletter, finding just the right mix of the following elements can make the newsletter something the family eagerly looks forward to reading.

Masthead

The masthead is also called the banner. This is the title of the newsletter. The masthead also contains the date the newsletter was created. You can keep the masthead simple, such as *The Jackson Family Newsletter* or play around with words to give your title a flashy flair such as the *Jackson Journal*. If you can't come up with a catchy title, experiment with fonts and type sizes to draw attention to the title. Fonts are the fancy way the letters look. Type size is how big or small the letters are.

The same information is made more dramatic just by experimenting with sizes and fonts. Word-processing software offers many kinds of typefaces, from simple to elaborate or from traditional to fun and funky. The style you use sets the tone for your entire newsletter.

Copy

Copy is the information that will make up the bulk of your newsletter. This information can cover a wide variety of topics, from reunion information to fun points of interest, such as the birth of a new family member or graduation announcements. For small newsletters, you may interview family members yourself. If your family members are local, a telephone call will give you all the information that you need. If you need to collect photographs, a visit may be in order.

If your family is widely scattered or if you are using a multipage format that requires more detail, you may rely on family members to submit story ideas and photographs to you. However you receive the information, try to follow the journalists' rule of writing: the five W's: who, what, why, when, and where an event occurred are usually answered in the first and second paragraphs.

Type

Type is a size or style of printed or typewritten characters. When you add copy, stick to one or two fonts and the same point size. Select a simple font such as Helvetica or Times Roman since these fonts are easy to read. When it comes to presenting information, less is more. The less elaborate the fonts are for the bulk of the newsletter, the more information your family will get out of it. If you must experiment with the copy, try using **boldface** or *italics*. These are subtle changes that will get the reader's attention and get your message across.

Graphics

Graphics are any nontext additions to the newsletter. This includes photographs, clip art, charts, and so on. If budget constraints are a concern, newsletters can be done in black and white. Also, for this reason, black-and-white photographs are the easiest with which to work. When they are photocopied, black-and-white pictures maintain more of their detail than a photocopied color photograph.

Paper

White is the standard for family newsletters. Other types of paper, such as color or glossy, give a more professional feel but are also more expensive. As a mid-priced alternative to plain white or colored paper, try using paper with a colored border.

If you decide to use anything other than standard paper for your newsletter, make sure your master copy is printed on white paper to ensure crisp, clean copies. The master is the original document, one that you will use to make other copies. If you use a master from colored paper, a grayish after image may appear on your copies.

Layout

Layout is the overall design of a page, spread, or book, including elements such as page and type size, typeface, and the arrangement of titles and page numbers.

Creating a Web Site

The Internet. World Wide Web. *Blah-blah-blah-dot-com.* The information superhighway is the latest phase in communication technology. A lot has been said and written about the Internet—some good, some bad. I like to call the Internet "cable TV for computers." There are so many choices, so many ways to get and send information through the Web. What you get out of it is what you expect to find.

You can use the Internet to your advantage. By creating a Web site, you can advertise the details of your family reunion, reaching potential family members not only across the country, but across the world.

There are five basic elements you need for creating your own family reunion Web site:

- A computer with a modem

- An active telephone line

- An Internet Service Provider (ISP)

- A software package, such as Microsoft Front Page, that allows you to create your Web page

- A Uniform Resource Locator (URL)

January '98   Issue #8

Jackson Family Newsletter
by Orlean Dorsey

Happy New Year!!

Hello family members. Another year has come and gone. And if you haven't done so already, you should stop and give thanks to the Lord for all your past blessings.

1998 promises to be an even greater year than the previous.

Family News

Vacation Tips #2

Traveling with little ones?....Better plan ahead advises specialist Emily Kaufman.

The golden rules:
- Load luggage the night before
- Get gas the night before
- Study directions

- Pack napkins, garbage bags & emergency supplies
  - Stop frequently and have a jump rope or frisbee to let off steam
- Pack some fun...
  - Cookie sheets with magnets
  - Froot Loops on a string
  - Books on tape
  - Road trip scavenger hunt
  - Disposable cameras
  - Egg carton with treats
- Other tips...
  - Grapes are hunger & thirst quenchers
  - Syrup bottles are great for all liquids
  - Dads, don't be guilty of getting too stuck in an agenda
  - Moms don't get swayed by wants not needs of the children
  - Don't have expectations, think of it as a change
  - Book another vacation for you and your spouse before or after
  - Give the kids a budget and let them help plan

- Bring stress reduction techniques ie. sneakers, knitting
- Negotiate driving duties ahead of time
- Have a strategy session ahead of time.

Remember: the main benefit is revitalization of family unity. And most importantly, understand that parents on vacation really aren't!

Get on The Bus

Beep beep. Although many of you will be making your own travel arrangements, several efforts are underway to arrange mass transportation from Texas to California.

Ulrica Fontenot has reserved a block of 30 seats with Continental Airlines and I've made arrangements to charter a 50-passenger bus from Lufkin to California by way of Houston and San Antonio.

We both are faced with the same dilemma. Many people expressed an interest and made a verbal commitment, but after using our credit cards to secure deposits, we have yet to here from hardly anybody.

So here's the deal...

GOOD SEATS ARE STILL AVAILABLE.

Computer

Due to the growing reliance on the Internet to exchange information, most computers produced these days come equipped with an internal modem. Modem speeds vary. Generally, the faster the modem, the faster you can access information from the Internet.

Telephone Line

Any standard residential telephone line used to connect your telephone will work with your computer. Computers with modems have a modem jack in which you plug one end of the telephone cord into the wall and the opposite end of the telephone cord into the modem jack of the computer. Test the modem using your computer's modem diagnostics software. If you hear a dial tone or if the software indicates that the modem line is connected, you have an active phone line.

I have a separate phone line that I only use with my computer. It is a no-frills line, without call-waiting or conference calling.

Internet Service Providers

The Internet is a computer network that connects millions of computers across the world. Internet Service Providers (ISP) offer the software necessary for you to access the Internet. Popular providers include companies such as America Online (AOL) or Netscape. For a monthly fee, they will grant unlimited access to the Internet, as well as provide other services, such as e-mail accounts and Web space, which is where you will keep the family reunion information you want to share with others.

Software for Creating the Web Page

Since there are so many different computers on the World Wide Web, all functioning differently, a common communication language had to be developed. Software packages, such as Microsoft Front Page, create files in a special language recognized by all of the different computers. This language is called HyperText Markup Language or HTML.

Software packages specifically for designing Web pages use easy-to-learn, familiar word-processing tools and graphics to help you determine how your Web page will look and work. However, behind the scenes is the HTML code that is recognized by the vast network of computers.

Uniform Resource Locator

The Uniform Resource Locator (URL) gives the location of the file on the World Wide Web and identifies the Internet service that provides it. An example of a URL might look like: *www.myfamilyreunionpage.com.* Once you have created a Web page using the HTML design software, contact your ISP. Your provider will issue a URL for you. To make certain that your special page can be found among millions of other pages on the Web, you can register it with Internet search engines.

Search engines are like automatic investigators. You type in a key word or phrase and the search engine will find all of the web sites containing that phrase. Popular search engines include Yahoo.com and AltaVista.com.

Elements of a Web Page

If you are using a Web page to advertise your family reunion, include all of the information you would in an invitation, such as the family name, the date and location of the reunion, how to make hotel reservations, and so on. You may also want to create a hyperlink to your e-mail address to get immediate feedback or comments. Hyperlinks are pointers to other sites of interest or specific e-mail addresses.

8

RECIPES FOR THE GENERATIONS

Where my grandmother lived there was
always sweet potato pie and thirds on
green beans.

—"#4" BY DOUGHTRY LONG

Home cookin'. Soul food. Comfort food. That's what I call the dishes that were prepared with loving hands by my grandmother. In preparation for our after-church dinners, she would wake at four or five o'clock in the morning to prepare the dishes that, if eaten today, would send my cholesterol level through the roof—fried chicken, rice and gravy, macaroni and cheese. Huge aluminum pans were filled with turkey wings and corn-bread dressing. Sheet cakes, with frosting melting deep into the crevices after being applied right out of the oven, would line the dining-room table.

Sometimes, I would sit and watch her cook, wondering how come she never measured seasonings. Yet everything always seemed to turn out just right. When I grew old enough to cook my own meals, I tried to duplicate some of those recipes. Somehow, they never came out quite right, even though I was sure I had gathered all of the ingredients I had seen her pull from her kitchen cabinets. My own meals never came out tasting exactly like my grandmother's. What was I missing?

My grandmother has seen a lot of pain in her life. She's also known a lot of joy. I wonder if it's possible that some of her life experience poured from her soul, through her hands, and into the food she prepared for us? Today, my grandmother is still going strong, still waking up in the wee hours of the morning to cook for her now great-great grandchildren. Even though they may watch her with as much care and curiosity, I'm sure they will be just as stymied as I was on how to re-create her comfort food. Sometimes I fear that when she's gone, the secret of her success will go to the grave with her.

In talking to several of my family reunion subject matter experts, they admitted having a hard time trying to get secret recipes out of their relatives, too. When you're searching for recipes, be persistent. Be gracious. Remind those jealously guarding the secret that their recipes are part of your heritage that should be shared with future generations. Use some of the same rigorous techniques for gathering family recipes that you did for going after your family roots. You may need to write a couple of pleading letters or call the ones who are late getting information back to you.

When family members find their recipes proudly displayed on the picnic and banquet tables or creatively entered into a beautiful keepsake, such as a family cookbook for everyont to enjoy, their praises will be the reward for all of the effort you put into gathering those recipes.

PLANNING A MENU

For a one-day event, such a picnic, planning a menu can be as simple as asking everyone to bring their own food. Each family would also be responsible for supplying their own drinks and utensils. Some public parks give access to barbecue grills; but you must supply your own charcoal and lighter fluid. As the reunion organizer, you may want to set up a "hospitality table" to include a few extras people may have forgotten, such as paper plates, plastic cutlery, napkins, cups, ice—don't forget garbage bags.

Even though allowing people to bring their own food saves the organizer time and money, it may hinder families getting together. If everyone is off with their own family, there is little incentive to get up and mingle.

One way of fostering family togetherness is for everyone to participate in a potluck. A potluck is where everyone brings a little something and sets it out on a table for all to share. Potlucks require a little more coordination as you want to make sure that there is a variety of foods on the table.

Another way to make sure that there is a variety of foods is for the reunion organizer to purchase and prepare the meat and provide drinks. Sodas offer more variety but iced tea is sometimes preferable since you can make iced tea by the gallon and you don't have to worry about cleaning up the cans after the reunion is over.

Family members would then supply the desserts and side dishes. When coordinating these dishes, use the reunion survey to contact relatives who said they would supply a dish. Make sure to give them a reminder notice a few days before the picnic to confirm what they will bring.

If no one is willing to cook, consider having the picnic catered. Fast-food restaurants can supply chicken (fried or barbecued) and salads can be picked up from delicatessens.

Multiday reunions, which include a picnic, follow the same guidelines. However, multiday events generally include a banquet, as well. A banquet is a formal affair, which will allow the family to share a meal. Banquets can be held at the hotel, restaurant, or other spaces that accommodate large groups of people such as a church hall or civic center.

Remember that meals at banquet halls are usually catered. The caterer provides a list of possible entrees such as beef, chicken, or fish.

Valerie Merlett, organizer of the Simmons Family Reunion, recalls, "We found our caterer through a local business exposition. It was an expo that focused on black businesses in the community. He agreed to cater the entire reunion for us at a special price if we agreed to give him exclusive rights to the entire reunion. That meant no running off somewhere to sneak in a box of chicken. The fun part about having the meal catered was that he prepared all of these delicious samples for us to try and we didn't have to cook."

When having a meal catered, make sure that there are enough choices for everyone. Remember to provide selections for those who may be on a low-fat diet or those who may be vegetarians.

SETTING UP A COOKBOOK MEMENTO

Cookbook mementos preserve favorite family recipes. Cookbooks can be done quickly, easily, and relatively inexpensively using a computer. Or, they can be elaborately bound works of art done professionally by a printer. Some family reunion organizers use the cookbook as a means of generating funds for the reunion. They prepare the cookbooks in advance of the family reunion and offer them for sale along with other keepsakes, such as T-shirts or hats. Or, they include the price of the cookbook in the registration fees or family dues.

When preparing a cookbook, decide early how recipe submissions will be accepted. Have some clearly established guidelines for submission. Let your family know the types of recipes you are looking for and the deadline for the recipes. If everyone knows the guidelines, you will not hurt anyone's feelings if their entries are not in the cookbook. For example, if you receive several entries for the same item, you can set a guideline stating the first entry received will be accepted. When you are collecting recipes, you may get several variations of your family favorite. How can you pick which recipe will go into the cookbook if the recipes are very similar?

It's hard to determine which is the best of all versions of a recipe. One way to generate interest in the cookbook is to hold a cooking contest. This works well for family members who live closely together. Or, you can have the contest during the reunion. Allow the family members to vote on the best recipes. The winning entries are placed in the cookbook to be mailed after the reunion is over.

If you have a large family (or even a small family with a deep love for cooking), gathering all of the family recipes can be a huge task in itself. One way to make the task easier is to spread the workload around. If you're the reunion organizer, appoint different family members to be responsible for each category in your family recipe book— such as desserts, main dishes, beverages, and so on. If you are organizing by committee, create a subcommittee specifically for the task of gathering recipes.

Ask family members to standardize recipes, including such specifics as precise baking times, oven temperature, and ingredient amounts. A recipe calling for "a pinch of this" and "handful of that" can come up with unexpected results. Instructions such as "cooked until done" can be confusing as well if you're not sure how *done* is supposed to appear.

Coordinate relatives for typing, proofreading, and illustrating the cookbook. Take advantage of each of your relatives' special skills. If you know of a relative who has a typewriter or computer, enlist that family member to help you type the recipes. If you have a relative who can draw, paint, or use calligraphy, ask that relative to help you illustrate the cookbook. Ask other relatives to test out the collected recipes before they're put into the cookbook.

When you start to gather the information for your recipe book, include the following information:

- Tie the old and the new together in a recipe book that includes old family favorites, especially recipes that have been passed down through the generations. You can also include a section for "Next Generation" recipes that have come into the family through marriages or through the next wave of culinary creativity.

- Any trivia, anecdotes, or family history surrounding the recipes.

- Reminisce about family members.

- Old family photos.

Try some of the following recipes out for yourself.

MAIN DISHES

Chicken Pot Pie

1 package frozen mixed vegetables
3 cups diced cooked chicken
1 16-ounce jar white sauce
2 medium potatoes, peeled, diced, and cooked
1 10-inch pie crust

Preheat the oven to 350°F.

Cook the vegetables according to package directions; drain. Add the chicken, white sauce, and potatoes and bring to a simmer.

Pour mixture into a 4-inch-deep pie pan and cover with the crust, cutting slits in the top.

Bake for 15 to 20 minutes or until golden brown.

Serves 4 to 6

Stewed Chicken

1 whole chicken, cut up (eight pieces)
1 green pepper, diced
1 red pepper, diced
1 medium onion, diced
1 green onion, diced
Salt, pepper, and paprika to taste
Water

Place all ingredients in a large saucepan with a little water (enough to keep the chicken from sticking to the pan, about 1 to 1½ cups). Cover and cook over low heat for 2 hours, or until chicken is no longer pink.

Serves 4

—Recipe from Ora L. Smith, 1998 Jackson Family Reunion

Tex-Mex BBQ Sandwich

Nonstick cooking spray
2 pounds beef round steak, trimmed of fat and cut into ¾ inch strips
1 14½-ounce can diced tomatoes, undrained
1 large onion, chopped
1 large carrot, chopped
2 tablespoons Worcestershire sauce
2 tablespoons vinegar
1 tablespoon brown sugar
2 teaspoons chili powder
2 tablespoons picante sauce
1 clove garlic, minced
1 bay leaf
8 hamburger buns

Spray the inside of a Dutch oven with nonstick cooking spray and heat. Add half of the steak pieces and brown on both sides. Set them aside and repeat with the remaining steak. Drain any fat and return all the steak to the pot.

Add the tomatoes, onion, carrot, Worcestershire sauce, vinegar, brown sugar, chili powder, picante sauce, garlic, and bay leaf. Bring to a boil, then reduce the heat. Cover and simmer for $2\frac{1}{2}$ hours or until the meat is very tender.

Remove the meat from the sauce and shred it. Simmer sauce uncovered for 7 to 10 minutes until slightly thickened. Discard the bay leaf.

Serve meat on buns topped with sauce.

Serves 8

—Recipe from Robert Livingston

SALADS

Pea Salad

1 8-ounce can peas, drained
1 8-ounce jar pimentos, diced
2 small dill pickles, diced
1 tablespoon fresh minced onion
4 tablespoons Cheddar cheese, diced
2 hard boiled eggs, peeled and diced
3 tablespoons mayonnaise

Combine all ingredients in a medium-sized bowl and chill for 1 hour.

Serves 4

—Recipe by Lucy M. Hall, from the *Westridge Park First Baptist Church Cookbook*

Fruit Salad

1 16-ounce can fruit cocktail
1 8-ounce can pineapple chunks
2 medium red apples, washed, peeled, cored, and diced
$\frac{1}{4}$ cup diced celery
$\frac{3}{4}$ cup miniature marshmallows
2 medium bananas, thinly sliced
$\frac{1}{3}$ cup plus 2 tablespoons mayonnaise
Peach slices and paprika (for garnish)

Drain the fruit cocktail and the pineapple, reserving the juice.

In a large bowl, combine the fruit cocktail, pineapple, apples, celery, marshmallows, bananas, and $\frac{1}{3}$ cup mayonnaise; stir lightly. In a separate bowl, combine 2 tablespoons of mayonnaise and $\frac{1}{3}$ cup of reserved juice; whisk thoroughly. Pour mayonnaise mixture over fruit and toss.

Chill, then serve on a bed of lettuce garnished with peach slices and paprika.

Serves 6

—Recipe by Maggie Duren from *The Westridge Park First Baptist Church Cookbook*

Side Dishes

Deviled Eggs

1 dozen hard boiled eggs
1 teaspoon Worcestershire sauce
1 red bell pepper, chopped
$\frac{1}{4}$ teaspoon onion salt
$\frac{1}{4}$ teaspoon garlic salt
2 tablespoons vinegar

2½ tablespoons mayonnaise
1 tablespoon prepared mustard
Creole seasoning and salt and pepper to taste
Paprika for garnish

Peel the eggs and cut them in half lengthwise. Remove the yolks and set the whites aside.

In a large bowl, mash the yolks with a fork. Add the bell pepper, onion and garlic salt, vinegar, mayonnaise, mustard, Creole seasoning, and salt and pepper; mix thoroughly.

Fill the egg white halves with the mixture and garnish with paprika. Chill for 1 hour.

Serves 12

Dirty Rice

2 8-ounce boxes wild rice
2 12-ounce cans clear chicken broth
4 cups water
2 tablespoons butter or margarine
2 cups white rice
1 cup chopped onions
1 cup chopped celery
2 pounds country-style hot sausage
2 8-ounce cans mushrooms, drained

Preheat oven to 325°F.

Cook the wild rice according to package directions, substituting the chicken broth for all or most of the water called for.

In a separate pot, bring the water to a boil and add the butter or margarine, white rice, onion, and celery. Cook, tightly covered, for 20 minutes or until the rice is tender and all of the water is absorbed.

While the rice is cooking, brown the sausage in a large skillet; drain.

Mix the two kinds of rice, the sausage, and the mushrooms in a medium-sized casserole dish and bake for 1½ hours.

Serves 6

—Recipe by Frank Butler in the *Westridge Park First Baptist Cookbook*

Rice and Okra Casserole

⅓ cup butter
1 medium onion, minced
½ pound okra, sliced
1 cup cooked wild rice
1 tablespoon curry powder
4 cups stewed tomatoes
Salt and pepper to taste

Preheat the oven to 350°F.

Melt the butter in a large saucepan. Add the onion and sauté until translucent. Stir in the okra, wild rice, curry powder, stewed tomatoes, and salt and pepper.

Place the vegetable mixture in a greased casserole dish, cover, and bake for 2 hours.

Serves 6

Stuffed Pork Chops

6 small (breakfast-style) pork chops
Salt and pepper to taste
1 14½-ounce can cream of mushroom soup
1 6-ounce box Stovetop stuffing

Preheat the oven to 300°F.

Season the pork chops with salt and pepper. In a skillet, brown the chops on both sides.

Place three of the chops in a casserole dish; place a layer of stuffing over them, then the three remaining chops on top of that, finishing with the remaining stuffing.

Mix the mushroom soup with a half can of water and pour over the mixture. Cover and bake for 25 minutes.

Serves 6

—Recipe from *The Westridge Park First Baptist Church Cookbook*

DESSERTS

Spicy Apple Loaf

1½ cups all-purpose flour
½ teaspoon baking soda
½ teaspoon ground cinnamon
¼ teaspoon baking powder
¼ teaspoon ground nutmeg
2 egg whites, beaten
¾ cup shredded apple peel
3 tablespoons cooking oil
½ teaspoon orange zest
½ teaspoon lemon zest
Nonstick cooking spray

Preheat the oven to 350°F.

In a small mixing bowl, stir together flour, baking soda, cinnamon, baking powder, and nutmeg. In a large mixing bowl, stir together the egg whites, brown sugar, apple peel, oil, and orange and lemon zests. Stir the flour mixture into the apple mixture.

Spray an 8 × 4 × 2-inch loaf pan with nonstick cooking spray and pour the batter into the pan.

Bake for 50 minutes or until a toothpick inserted into the middle of the loaf comes out clean. Cool the bread in the pan for 10 minutes. Remove loaf from the pan and continue to cool on a wire rack.

Makes 1 loaf

—Recipe from Donna Dorsey

Strawberry Whip

1 cup fresh or frozen strawberries, thawed, washed, and drained
1 3-ounce package strawberry flavored gelatin
1 cup boiling water
$^2/_3$ cup cold water
$^1/_4$ teaspoon ground nutmeg
1 8-ounce carton vanilla low-fat yogurt

Dissolve the gelatin in the boiling water in a large bowl, following the package instructions. Add the cold water, stirring constantly. Cover and chill for about 40 minutes, or until the gelatin is partially set.

Fold the yogurt into the gelatin mixture. Beat with an electric mixer on medium for 1 to 2 minutes, or until the mixture is light and frothy.

Divide half the strawberries among 6 dessert dishes. Spoon the gelatin mixture on top, and garnish with the remaining strawberries.

Chill an additional 30 minutes, or until firm
Serves 6

—Recipe from Donna Dorsey

9

ACTIVITIES FOR ALL

Calling black people
Calling all black people, man woman child
—"SOS" by Imamu Amiri Baraka (LeRoi Jones)

1-2-3-4-5-6-7-8-9-10! *Ready or not, here I come!* It was your last warning to scatter before the ones who were "It" uncovered their eyes and chased you from your hiding places. Hide-and-seek, Freeze Tag, Not It, and other childhood chase games filled my summer days while growing up in my grandmother's house in Mississippi. It didn't matter to me and my multitude of cousins that it was a hundred and two degrees in the shade. School was out and we were ready to fill the days with as much fun as we could cram into the long, hot days.

When planning activities for your family reunion, you want to find just the right balance. If you plan too many activities, you may tire out your relatives. Or, you may overwhelm them with so many things to do that they end up doing very little. You can also under-plan activities. This leaves the door open for boredom. If family members are bored and dissatisfied, they may not attend the next reunion. Having a wide variety of activities that appeal to almost every family member gives everyone the opportunity to enjoy themselves.

If organizing for a picnic reunion, whether your reunion is a single day or spans a weekend, keep in mind some of the following guidelines:

PLANNING FOR THE PICNIC

Hosting a picnic is one of the most common means of gathering the family together for one, fun-filled day. A relaxed, open area provides the perfect setting for encouraging family members to either kick back and relax or get in on the fun of some of the preplanned events. When planning a picnic reunion, certain details must be taken into consideration. All of these details should be put into place before the day of the reunion.

Weather

You can plan a picnic to the nth degree, but you can't do anything about the weather. If you're planning a one-day event and the weather doesn't cooperate, have a contingency plan in place. You can either move the entire reunion to a different location or you can hold the reunion another day.

Moving to a different location is the easiest alternative. To make allowances for bad weather, preselect a location that will accommodate the number of people you expect to attend your reunion. For example, you don't want a hundred relatives crammed into a small restaurant. Church halls usually have the facilities to accommodate large groups. Make arrangements with the church administrators. Let them know how many people you expect to use the facility and for how long. It's usually easier to gain access to the church where one family member is an active attendee. Contact the church's administrative office.

Another option is for reunion organizers to plan a rain day. A rain day is an alternate day selected to hold events if the weather interferes. A rain day alternate works well if most family members are in a central location, such as the same city. If you must postpone your reunion, try to have the rain day in the same weekend. Family members who have used vacation time to attend your reunion may not have additional time if the rain day is scheduled for the next weekend.

A rain day that occurs during a multiday event means that you will not have time to do all of the activities planned. Something will have to be cut. Decide in advance which activities will be eliminated in order to make room for the remaining events.

Whatever contingency plan you choose, make sure that your family members know what the plan is. Include the contingency-plan information in the registration packets.

Cancellation of the entire reunion, if the event is a one-day event, is the most drastic option. You don't want to face disgruntled family members who have spent time and money to attend. If you know that the area you reserved for the reunion is sheltered, you may want to consider going through with the reunion. There's something to be said for togetherness. Get a consensus from the family before canceling the event that took so long to plan.

Site

Many reunion picnics are held in public parks. Some parks require a permit. If you are planning by committee, the reunion-site selection committee is responsible for getting the necessary paperwork in place in time for the reunion. Public parks don't usually require a permit. This makes them very popular for weekend events such as family reunions. In order to get a prime location, family members should arrive at the park early to claim an area. Covered park areas are especially popular.

When selecting a park, keep in mind some of the following guidelines:

Is the Park Easy to Locate?

Take a trial run from the hotel to the park site using the map you will provide to the site. Are the directions easy to follow? Have you left off any major landmarks that will help your family members along the way? Because you may be familiar with the site, you may be able to find it without mistakes. Get a volunteer who has not been to the site to test the directions.

Is There Adequate Parking and Lighting for After-Dark Activities?

The only way to find out about the lighting is to be at the park after the sun goes down. Assuming twenty-twenty vision, can you clearly see objects twenty feet from you? Ten? Less than ten feet in front of you may present a hazard. You want to keep your family members free from accidents and from those who may take advantage of a single relative wandering in the dark.

If you do not feel the lighting is adequate, you will need a generator and a string of lights to keep the environment fun and safe. Don't forget to purchase extra bulbs in case some of the bulbs are broken while stringing them or blow out during the reunion. You will also need heavy-duty orange extension cords that are especially made for outdoor use. Check the UL (United Laboratories) label to ensure that the extension cord is rated for outdoor use.

Is There Enough Room for the Children to Run and Play?

At a picnic, the children are going to be seen *and* heard. Their laughter and their capacity for fun adds spirit and smiles to the occasion. There will be plenty of time for the children to sit still during the meals. Make sure there is enough space for them to run freely without bumping into the tables, generators, or cooking grills.

Are There Adequate Restroom Facilities at the Site?

If not, arrange to have a portable toilet and adequate supplies of tissue on hand. There are companies that rent portable toilets. Look in the yellow pages under "Toilets-Portable" or the reverse, "Portable-Toilets". Even if there are public restrooms at your chosen reunion site, they may not be as well-stocked as you'd like. Be prepared in any eventuality.

Activities

After you've taken so much care and effort into getting your relatives together, you don't want them to remain rooted to their seats or mingle only with those family members they know. If you are organizing the reunion through a committee, the program committee is responsible for making certain that the activities are designed to help your family get reacquainted. Chapter 12 will provide examples of games that will suit all ages.

Generally, activities will either require lots of energy (such as sports) or, they will require exercise of the mind (such as chess, checkers, or dominoes). Sporting-good stores, such as Oshman's or general-merchandise stores such as Wal-Mart provide equipment for games such as volleyball, baseball, or horseshoes. The general-merchandise stores are also sources of low-cost games that do not require physical activity, such as checkers, Monopoly, Uno, and so on. I like to have five sets or types of board games for every fifteen to twenty relatives. If I happen to misjudge the number of relatives who are interested in playing a certain game, I provide a timer and set it around twenty minutes. When the timer is up, the players are done. Of course, you can always ask relatives to bring their own games if they don't want to share.

For the children, I shop the bargain or everything-a-dollar stores for such items as rubber balls, water balloons, dolls, and Frisbees. As you purchase each item, include that item on the activities' checklist. You will use this checklist later on the reunion day to make certain these items are at the picnic site.

REMEMBRANCES OF REUNIONS PAST:
MARY LIVINGSTON, JACKSON FAMILY REUNION, 1997

Our family thrives on a domino tournament. The activities committee sets up tables early in the morning and the games usually run well into the night. *I* can't play dominoes to save my life. Knowing that the reunion committee also provided playing cards, Frisbees, and even fishing poles for fishing gave me a choice of activities requiring heavy, physical exertion or quiet time.

Food

Plain and simple, the food makes the picnic. When all of your relatives have batted their last ball, bingoed their last bingo, or boogied their last boogie, they will be ready to sit back and enjoy a well-prepared repast.

If you're having a one-day event, the easiest way to make sure everyone is well-fed is to require that they bring their own lunch. This requires less organization for you and your committees.

Or, to encourage the spirit of family togetherness, you can have a potluck picnic. This may be a little difficult when hosting a reunion for several hundred family members.

Music

Music can set the mood for a reunion picnic. Music that is too loud, or placed too closely to where the family congregates will hinder conversation. Music that is too soft or too monotonous can dull the active edge. Remember, after a good meal, the temptation to lie under one of those park shade trees can work against any other activities you have planned.

To get a feel for your relatives' taste and preferences for styles of music, include the question in the reunion survey you originally sent. If you get varied responses about music style, you can keep the reunion picnic lively and entertaining.

Once you have an idea of what kind of music your family is interested in, hire a deejay. Deejays can be found in the yellow pages. Or, you can contact local nightclubs or radio stations for popular deejays. Remember, since they are the more popular deejays, their price per hour may be more than your budget can accommodate. As an alternative, you can check out the bulletin boards of local colleges or universities. Nestled among the term-paper-typing-for-hire notices, you will find ads for college students looking to pick up a few extra dollars. Or, maybe you have a wealth of talent right in your own family. If you have family members who are musically talented, ask them to perform.

You won't be able to please everyone with the musical choices. However, you can follow certain guidelines to reduce the number of complaints.

● Keep the music selection upbeat and positive.

● Stay away from songs that may contain graphic or offensive language.

● Rotate the various musical styles so that everyone gets a chance to enjoy their preferences.

Whether you decide to go with a professional deejay or an aspiring one, make sure that you listen to the selection of titles before the reunion to get an idea of what the deejay intends to play. I find that "tasteful music" is too vague a term when interviewing deejays. Tastes vary.

Security

You want your family reunion to be a memorable event—but not because a family member met with an unfortunate incident. We live in dangerous times. However, you don't have to let an unseen threat spoil your special day. When scheduling services for your family reunion, such as a deejay or trash pickup, consider hiring a peace officer for the day. The peace officer will patrol the grounds to protect your most valued possessions—your family. Contact your local police department or patrolman's union. Off-duty officers sometimes supplement their income (with the police department's approval) with private-security duties. The security officer you select should be:

- Warm and personable, yet professional. Some family members, including children, have a fear and distrust of peace officers. You want your relatives to feel comfortable and secure when the security officer patrols the grounds. The security officer is there to prevent incidents, not instigate them.

- Wearing a uniform on the day of the event. The peace officer should be immediately recognizable as such. If the officer is dressed in plain clothes on the day of the reunion, you don't want to waste precious moments searching among your similarly dressed relatives.

- In good health. Having a figurehead as a security guard—one that only has a uniform and who is not in good physical condition—will not likely deter crime. When interviewing candidates, ask yourself, does this person look capable of defending me or my family from assailants?

Cleanup

A cleanup detail can be arranged in two ways. You can pre-select family members before the reunion. A phone call to my environmentally active relatives is usually enough to set up a team in advance. You can also recruit volunteers on the day of the reunion to make sure that all trash is placed in its proper receptacles.

We can do our part to help the environment by keeping specialized containers for recycling in strategic locations around the picnic site. Small recycling bins can be purchased at general-merchandise stores. If you foresee a huge amount of waste, recycling companies will pick up at a reduced fee or even for free.

REMEMBRANCES OF REUNIONS PAST: *ORLEAN L. DORSEY, JACKSON FAMILY REUNION, 1998*

In 1998, we decided for the first time to have the family reunion at a location other than our family homestead in Lufkin, Texas. We chose Los Angeles, California, because most of our relatives have migrated there. I was really looking forward to going to California, mainly to visit my two aunts (Addie Rudolph and Ora Jackson) who live there. I was also excited about not having to coordinate anything. In the past, my biggest complaint was that I would organize all these activities and people would march to the beat of their own drummer. As it turned out, my cousin Ulrica, her husband, George, and I spent so much energy devoted to planning flight arrangements, trips to Disneyland, Hollywood, Magic Mountain, and other places, we missed several of the activities planned by our relatives. It was very ironic that I worked harder that weekend than I ever had at previous reunions.

MULTIDAY EVENT

A picnic is usually part of a multiday event, so please feel free to use any of the above suggestions. Because a weekend reunion requires more details, you give the event a sense of coordination and unity if you apply a specific theme.

Themes

When events are spread across several days, a common theme all of the events together will give your reunion the look and feel of unity. Some popular themes include:

Passing the Torch

At each stage of the family reunion, we must never forget that the young children we see running, laughing, and sometimes crying before us will someday be our future leaders. They will grow up to become our presidents, teachers, and doctors. They will become our next generation of mothers and grandmothers. Use the family reunion as a vehicle for passing on our knowledge and experiences.

Family Links

Looking at the faces around you, and being able to point out the parents of Cousin so-and-so or the children of Brother so-and-so is a constant reminder of how we are all connected. You have made the effort to assemble because you believe in preserving the family. "Linking" them connects the memories of our ancestors with the potential of our posterity.

10

KEEPSAKES AND
MEMENTOS

My love has left me, has gone from me
And I with no keepsake nothing
—"SOUVENIRS" BY DUDLEY RANDALL

Memories may be long or they may be fleeting. The funny thing about memories is that no two individuals remember a shared event the same way. One way to make certain that your family's memories, traditions, and heritage are preserved is to provide keepsakes. Some keepsakes, such as T-shirts are distributed during the reunion. And, on an appointed day, everyone wears the shirts. Other keepsakes, such as group photographs and memory books, are distributed after the reunion.

Long after the last meal is digested and the final notes of the picnic music have faded, keepsakes provide a constant reminder of the love and kinship that you shared during the communion with your relatives. Keepsakes should say something special about your family—because they are reminders of who you are.

ITEMS IMPRINTED WITH THE FAMILY LOGO

Some popular keepsakes for family reunions include T-shirts, hats, buttons, or aprons imprinted with a family logo or motto. Popular logos for keepsake items include trees, to represent the deep roots and wide branches of your extended family. If your family reunion is centered around a theme, select a logo that embodies that theme. For example, Orlean Dorsey hosts several reunions in Texas. The cowboy is a popular image associated with Texas. When ordering these keepsakes, keep in mind some of the following guidelines:

- Use the information gathered by your pre-reunion survey to estimate how many items you will need, such as T-shirts, and in which sizes.

- When contacting companies to print up your keepsakes, remember that the more that you order, the better price per item you are likely to get.

- Order items far enough in advance so that they will be ready for the reunion. Ask the supplier for a reasonable return date, then add on at least a week of extra time to make allowances for unforeseen events.

- Shop around to get the best price. When comparing quotes, make certain that you are comparing apples to apples. For example, a price quoted for a shirt with a fifty-fifty blend of cotton and polyester will not be the same price as the price quote for a pure, cotton shirt or all polyester material.

  Keep in mind, in the summer months, cotton is cooler. The material breathes more. Cotton and polyester blends are more resilient. They hold the original color and shape better. Be clear what you are looking for when talking to the supplier.

- When ordering your keepsakes, take into account any major events that may be happening in the city. For example, if the reunion is scheduled near a major holiday, your order may be delayed so that the supplier can meet the higher demand. If your order is delayed, ask for a special discounted price in restitution.

- Don't be afraid to ask for references. Make sure to check the references, as well. Satisfied customers will give glowing reports of the service. However, you can expect that the supplier will not give you the name of a customer who won't give a favorable report. So, check other sources of information as well. A good rule of thumb when dealing with any supplier of a service or merchandise is to check with the Better Business Bureau (BBB). If there are formal complaints filed against the company, don't use that service.

Photographs

Photographs are a reflection of our personal histories. In order to preserve the history of your family reunion, take plenty of photographs. They can be candid, unplanned, and unposed shots. These images are usually the most fun, catching the family member off-guard in a moment of high action, such as in the middle of a sack race, unrestrained laughter, or bittersweet tears. Or, the photographs can be orchestrated or staged, with groups of family members lined up especially for the camera.

To make sure the full scope and spirit of the family reunion is captured, have several family members canvas the reunion, catching everyone with their electronic camera eyes. The more photos, the greater the memories.

Or, if the budget allows, you may want to hire a professional photographer. This will free up your family members to participate in the fun they would miss if they were taking photos.

Some family reunions are so large, that all family members cannot be photographed at one time. To make sure that everyone is included in your family album, schedule photography sessions, in which different family members appear at an appointed time to have their photograph taken. The schedule should be included in the registration packet.

Types of Cameras

There are several types of cameras on the market, designed to meet every budget and photograph-taking ability.

Funsaver cameras from Kodak provide an integrated solution to taking pictures. They are disposable cameras sold with the film already inside. These cameras are easy to operate; you don't have to worry about focusing or changing lenses. When you have snapped the last shot, simply take the entire camera to a location that develops film. Prices for disposable cameras usually run about $5 to $10 and can be purchased at local grocery or drugstores.

OneStep instant cameras by Polaroid or similar camera manufacturers allow you to view pictures almost instantly. Film loading is simple. Install a cartridge into the front of the camera. These types of cameras provide immediate picture development. Prices of these cameras range from $30 to $50, not including the price of the film. An advantage to using this type of camera is seeing instant results. A disadvantage of these types of photographs is their short shelf life. Even with advanced camera and film technology, these pictures can begin to fade sooner than pictures taken with 35 millimeter (mm) film.

Manufactured by companies such as Minolta, 35mm cameras provide a higher-quality photograph. Because of the higher selections of film quality, you can be assured that photographs taken now will be around in thirty years without losing their quality. These cameras are more sophisticated. With the advent of drop-in film loading and multiple lenses within a single photo, you pay a higher price for making the technology simplistic. These cameras can range anywhere from $80 to $150.

Digital cameras, which store the camera image as a file that can be manipulated using a computer, are the next wave of photography. The images from digital cameras can be used in your newsletters or printed on silk screen for your keepsakes such as T-shirts or buttons. Because the technology is still fresh and new, purchasing a digital camera for your family reunion may be a little out of your price range. However, some camera shops are willing to rent the equipment.

Panoramic cameras are used for taking wide shots, such as group pictures, which will include the entire family. Again, this is a specialty camera. The purchase of this camera may be an unnecessary expense for one day. If you hire a professional photographer and you want a formal group picture, ask if the photographer has access to a panoramic camera.

One fun note about panoramic cameras is how they work. Some panoramic cameras operate by sweeping one end of the area, moving slowly to the opposite end. If you are on the end of one side, it's possible to run around the back of the group and position yourself on the opposite end of the picture before the camera stops moving. When the picture is developed, you'll see yourself on both ends. Just remember to let the photographer know in advance if you're going to try something like this. It's less disruptive to the picture-taking process. The photographer can tell you the best time to "cut and run."

Caring for Photographs

Color photographs are more eye-catching in a family album. However, their life expectancy is roughly forty to fifty years.

Black-and-white photographs last longer. If you are preserving the breadth and scope of the family using photographs, use a combination of both color and black-and-white photos to ensure the generations to follow can connect themselves to the faces proudly displayed in the photo albums. To preserve your family's photo history, use the highest quality photo film, paper, and album.

Use blank stickers available at office-supply stores to place in the photo albums next to each photo. Use these stickers to number the photos. As you go through each photo, make a note of who is in the picture and the date. Include this information on a summary sheet. The information doesn't have to be detailed, just a memory jogger. Having the summary sheet included with the photo helps to recall those fleeting memories when you flip back through the pages of the photo album and reminisce on the good times you had at your reunion.

VIDEO CAMERAS

Video cameras also come in various sizes and price ranges. They are an excellent method of capturing the moment. They provide the sights and the sounds with enough startling clarity to make you feel as if you were reliving the moment. Use the video camera to create a live-action documentary of your family reunion.

REMEMBRANCES OF REUNIONS PAST:
DONNA WHITE, WHITE FAMILY REUNION, JULY 1997

At the end of every reunion, we try to recognize the contributions of our family members for all of their hard work. For our fifteenth annual family reunion, my cousin who works at Xerox corporation, supplied all of the huge outside signs and banners. We honored her contribution by giving her a plaque as a token of our appreciation. A couple of weeks later, she presented us a beautifully bound book that included a retrospective of our family history, samples of our favorite family poems, reunion program, and enlarged photographs of some of the activities.

Orlean L. Dorsey, Jackson Family Reunion, June 1996

We sell T-shirts to raise money for our family reunion. One year, we thought we'd make the keepsakes extra special. We gave everyone T-shirts with their own name on it. Everyone was excited to get these personalized shirts. But you have to be careful when making an item too personal. In order to have the shirts made in time for the reunion, I had to have them ordered, made, and paid for well in advance. And if anyone doesn't pay for their shirt, you may be stuck with it. To keep the shirts generic enough for anyone to wear and still make a little money on them, we try to order shirts of different designs and colors for each reunion.

Valerie Merlett, Simmons Family Reunion, 1997

We wanted a keepsake that really meant something to the family. We always did T-shirts. I have a whole drawerful of T-shirts. But, when I was planning my family reunion, I really wanted to do something that the family would remember. We decided to do a calendar. My grandmother had twelve children. We highlighted one child each month of the year.

11

PREPARING FOR EMERGENCIES

Stop jumping on the bed! In the hotel room during one of my first family reunions, my three-year-old daughter decided to turn her bed into a trampoline. Before I could tell her to stop, she'd flipped off the edge of the bed and onto the nightstand beside it, which resulted in a three-inch gash in her forehead. Her howls of pain and dismay, anger at myself for not being more watchful, and other factors added to my feelings of helplessness. I was in an unfamiliar city. My husband had taken the car to visit with other relatives at the reunion site. Even if I'd been able to drive, where was I going to go? I didn't know the location of the nearest hospital and neither did the hotel staff. What was I going to do?

Careful planning of your reunion goes a long way toward making sure that events run smoothly. However, you cannot plan for every contingency. Despite all of your careful preparations, checks, and double-checks, sometimes accidents happen.

You may not be able to prevent all accidents. However, you can be equipped to handle emergencies promptly and effectively to prevent them from turning into tragedies. The suggestions for accident preparation in this chapter are not substitutes for the care of qualified medical doctors or emergency medical technicians, such as paramedics. The suggested treatments for injuries in this chapter are basic and should be confirmed by the American Red Cross.

BEFORE-REUNION PREPARATIONS

First Aid Training

First aid, according to *The American Heritage Dictionary,* is the emergency treatment administered to an injured or sick person before professional medical care is available. First aid includes recognizing when conditions could be life-threatening, then taking action to prevent death or further injury, relieving pain, counteracting shock, and transporting the victim to obtain any necessary medical treatment.

When forming committees or recruiting volunteers to help with your family reunion planning efforts, try to identify a select few to serve as first-aid experts. You will want to choose individuals who are calm in the face of chaos. They must be able to assess a situation quickly and administer the proper aid.

To help prepare these individuals to conquer emergency situations, consider enrolling them into first-aid training classes. One of the key training classes for your first-aid experts should be cardiopulmonary resuscitation (CPR). CPR is an emergency procedure, often employed after cardiac arrest, in which cardiac massage, artificial respiration, and drugs are used to maintain the circulation of oxygenated blood to the brain.

For CPR training, look to your area hospital or clinic community outreach efforts. In addition to free or reduced-fee immunizations, tips on proper eating habits, and cholesterol screenings, CPR training classes may also be offered. Charitable organizations such as the Red Cross or Young Men's Christian Association (YMCA) can also be sources of this life-saving training.

For health-awareness campaigns, some local government agencies will also provide CPR training. Once or twice a year, the city of Houston, Texas, offers a one-day training session on the basics of CPR. Hundreds of people are gathered in one area and given access to equipment and information that may help them someday save a life.

Basics of CPR

When preparing to give CPR, you must take into account the differences between adults and children. These are some CPR steps to take when administering to adults:

1. *Call 911.*

2. *Check the person for unresponsiveness.* Call the person by name or shake gently.

3. *Check for breathing.* Position the person flat on his or her back. Kneel by his or her side and place one hand on the forehead and the other under the chin. Tilt the head back and lift the chin until the teeth almost touch. Look and listen for breathing.

4. *Give two breaths.* If not breathing normally, pinch the nose and cover the mouth with yours. Give two full breaths. The person's chest will rise if you are giving enough air.

5. *Check the pulse.* Put the fingertips of your hand on the person's Adam's apple, slide your fingers into the groove next to the windpipe. Feel for a pulse. If you cannot feel a pulse or if you are unsure, move on to the next step.

6. *Position your hands* in the center of the chest between the nipples. Place one hand on top of the other.

7. *Pump fifteen times.* Push down firmly two inches. Push on chest fifteen times. Continue with two breaths and

fifteen pumps. Alternate chest compressions and breaths until help arrives or until breathing returns.

Basic CPR Steps for Children

CPR for children is similar to performing standard CPR for adults.

1. If you are alone with the child, give one minute of CPR before calling 911.

2. Use the heel of one hand for chest compressions.

3. Press the sternum or breastbone down one to one and a half inches.

4. Give chest compressions at the rate of 100 per minute.

5. Give one full breath followed by five chest compressions. Repeat until help arrives or until pulse returns.

Basic CPR Steps for Infants

1. Gently shake the child on the shoulder. If there is no response, position the infant on his or her back

2. Open the airway using a head-tilt lifting of chin. Do not tilt the head too far back.

3. Give two breaths. If the baby is *not* breathing, give two small, gentle breaths. Cover the baby's mouth and nose with your mouth. Each breath should be one and a half to two seconds long. You should see the baby's chest rise with each breath.

4. Locate a pulse. Try to feel for a pulse in the inside of the upper arm. If there is no pulse, proceed to next step.

5. Give five gentle chest compressions at the rate of 100 per minute. Position your third and fourth fingers in the center of the baby's chest half an inch below the nipples. Press down only half an inch to one inch.

6. Repeat with one breath and five compressions. After one minute of repeated cycles, call 911. If you feel a pulse return, give one breath every three seconds and discontinue chest compressions.

During-Reunion Preparations

Set up a booth where your first-aid experts will be visible and available to help. At the booth, keep the following items in your first-aid kit

- Absorbent cotton
- Ace bandage
- Adhesive tape
- Antihistamines
- Aspirin, acetaminophen, or ibuprofen
- Calamine lotion
- Cotton swaps
- Disposable rubber gloves
- Flashlight
- Hydrogen peroxide
- Large safety pins
- Large scarf or handkerchief
- Liquid disinfectant soap
- Liquid pain reliever for children
- Rolls and packages of gauze
- Scissors
- Syrup of ipecac (to induce vomiting)

- Thermometers

- Tweezers

Keep a fully charged cellular telephone to contact 911. Once you determine the nature of the accident, give the 911 operator as much information about the situation as you can.

The following are some types of injuries and methods for treating them until help arrives. The injured person may show any one or all of these symptoms. Knowing what to look for will help you determine how to treat them. The more information you can give the 911 operator and the EMTs, the faster they will be able to aid the injured person.

Bleeding/Shock

If the person is bleeding or shows signs of going into shock, try to determine:

- If the person is breathing.

- If the person has a heartbeat.

- The site of the bleeding.

- The cause of the bleeding (for example, due to an accident or fight).

- Whether the bleeding is an even flow or spurting.

Complete the following actions:

- Apply direct pressure and elevation to the bleeding site.

- Stay calm.

- Lie the person down with their legs elevated.

- Keep the person warm.

- Perform CPR, if necessary.

Fracture/Broken Bone

If the person has a fracture or broken bone, try to determine:

- The injury site.
- The history of the incident (for example, fell from ladder, tripped over an object).
- If the broken bone is protruding through the skin.
- If there is any bleeding.
- If the person is short of breath.
- If the person is complaining of back pain or no sensation in arms or legs.

Complete the following actions:

- Do not move the person unless there is immediate danger.
- If it is necessary to move the person, splint the fractured limb.
- *Do not* attempt to straighten the fractured limb or to position an exposed bone under the skin.
- Place a supportive object such as a pillow at the person's affected side.

No Breathing

If the person is not breathing, try to determine:

- If the person is conscious.
- If the person is cyanotic (turning blue).
- If the person is wheezing.

- If the person is experiencing any numbness or tingling in their hands or mouth.

- If the person is experiencing any chest pain.

- The person's age.

Complete the following actions:

- If the person is not breathing, perform CPR.

- If the person is experiencing chest pain, see the section on Chest Pain.

- Have the person sit up or sit in the most comfortable position.

Head, Neck, and Spine Injuries

For injuries to the head, neck, or spine, try to determine:

- The cause of the injury.

- If the person is conscious.

- If the person is breathing.

- If the person has a heartbeat.

- If there is any bleeding from the person's mouth, nose, ears, or open wounds.

- If the person is alert.

- If the person is experiencing any pain in the neck or numbness or tingling in extremities.

- If the person is vomiting.

- What position the person is in.

Complete the following actions:

- Do not move the person.

- Do not use any twisting motion to the person's head, neck, or spine.

- Keep the person's head, neck, and spine aligned. If possible, restrict movement.

- Do not stop blood flow from nose or ears.

- Apply direct pressure to bleeding wounds.

- Maintain the person's airway. (If vomiting, keep the airway clear.)

Burns

For burns, try to determine:

- If anything is still burning.
- If the person is still smoldering.
- If the person is breathing.
- If the person has a heartbeat.
- The extent of the burns.
- The part(s) of the person that are burned.

Complete the following actions:

- If still burning, roll the person in a blanket or coat, or douse with water.
- Remove burning or smoldering clothing.
- If possible, remove from smoky area.
- Assess breathing, heartbeat.
- Perform mouth-to-mouth resuscitation or CPR, if needed.
- Cool burns in water.

- Do not apply ointments such as grease, butter, etc.
- Wash injury with water if chemicals are involved.

Chest Pain

If the person is experiencing chest pain, try to determine:

- If the person is conscious.
- If the person is breathing.
- If the person is turning blue.
- If the person is short of breath.
- If the person has a heartbeat.
- If the person is exhibiting pain. If so, what kind of pain and where is it?
- If the person can describe the pain. (Is it sharp? Dull? Does the pain radiate anywhere?)
- If the person has a history of heart problems.
- If the person has a fever or cough.
- If the person is sweaty or nauseated.

Complete the following actions:

- Lie the person down in a semi-reclining position.
- Calm and reassure the person.

Stroke

In case of a stroke, try to determine:

- If the person is conscious.
- If the person is breathing.

- If the person has a heartbeat.
- If the person is alert.
- The person's age.
- What was the onset of symptoms?

Complete the following actions:

- Clear the airway.
- Do not put pillows behind the person's head.
- Lie the person down or place in a semi-reclining position.
- Perform mouth-to-mouth or CPR, if needed.

Seizures

In cases of seizures, try to determine:

- If the person is conscious.
- If the person is breathing.
- If the person has a heartbeat.
- If the seizure has stopped.
- If the person has a history of seizures.
- If trauma preceded the seizure.
- The person's age.
- If the person is pregnant.
- If the person has a fever.

Complete the following actions:

- Check to see if the person is breathing.

- Do not perform CPR while the person is still convulsing.

- Do not restrain the person if still convulsing.

- Do not put anything in the person's mouth.

- Move dangerous objects away from the person.

- Turn the person gently to the side after the seizure stops. Allow the person to rest.

- Do not allow the person to wander after the seizure stops.

- Reassure the person.

- If the person is conscious or sleeping, do not disturb.

Choking

In cases of choking, try to determine:

- If the person is still choking.

- If the person is conscious.

- If the person can speak or cough.

- The person's age.

- What caused the choking.

- If the person is standing, sitting, or lying down.

Complete the following actions:

- Calm and reassure the person.

- Make sure the person is unable to talk or cough before trying to remove the object.

Removing an Obstruction

If the person can walk or stand

1. Bring the person near the phone while speaking with the 911 dispatcher.

2. Turn the person away from you. Support the person's chest with one hand and arm.

3. Put your arms around the person and place one fist over stomach with knuckle of thumb tucked into fist and thumb facing toward person's stomach. Place your fist halfway between the waist and ribs.

4. Perform the Heimlich Maneuver: Clasp one fist with the other hand and jerk inward and up into the person's stomach up to five times. Repeat steps 1 through 4 until the person expels the object or becomes unconscious.

If the person is unconscious

1. Place the person face up.

2. Establish unresponsiveness by trying to shake the person awake, if you did not witness the incident. If they do not respond, continue with step 3.

3. Tilt the head back. Pinch the nose closed with thumb and forefinger, and force two slow breaths into the person.

4. If the chest does not rise, tilt the head and try again.

5. Put heel of one hand on person's stomach halfway between belly button and ribs. Then place the other hand on top of the first hand.

6. Press into the stomach with a quick upward thrust up to five times. If object pops loose, remove it and see if

person is able to breathe. If the object does not pop loose, open airway and perform finger sweep and attempt to give mouth-to-mouth.

7. Repeat abdominal-thrust procedure up to five times, open airway and perform finger sweep and attempt to give mouth-to-mouth. Keep repeating this sequence until the ambulance arrives.

To Remove an Object from a Choking Infant:

1. Place the infant face down straddling your forearm with head lower than body.

2. Give up to five quick back blows between the infant's shoulder blades.

3. Place free hand on the infant's back, holding the infant's head. Turn baby over. Place baby across thigh with baby's head lower than body.

4. Perform up to five quick downward chest thrusts by placing two fingers on lower third of breastbone just below nipple line. Open airway and attempt to give mouth-to-mouth resuscitation.

5. Repeat the entire sequence of opening the infant's airway, attempting to breathe, and performing up to five-quick thrusts until the ambulance arrives.

Eye Injuries

In cases of eye injuries, try to determine:

● Type of accident.

● If the object is still in the eye.

● Type or name of chemical agent.

- If the eyeball is bleeding or cut.
- If there is an impaled object.

Complete the following actions:

- Lie the person down on his back.
- If there is a chemical in the eye, flush immediately with water until arrival of the ambulance. Pour—don't squirt—water directly on the eye from inner to the outer corner.
- If there is a foreign body in the eye, do not attempt to remove it. If the object is large (such as a stick or knife), support the object with bandages. *Do not* dislodge it.

Poisoning

In cases of poisoning, try to determine:

- If the person is conscious.
- If the person is breathing.
- If the person has a heartbeat.
- The person's age.
- What and how much was ingested?
- When was the poison ingested?

Complete the following actions:

- If the person is unconscious, place on their left side, if possible.
- Perform mouth-to-mouth or CPR, if needed.
- Gather medicines or bottles to help paramedics identify what was ingested.

- If anticipated response time is less than ten minutes, do not treat until help arrives.

- If vomiting, save the vomitus.

Unconsciousness

If the person is unconscious, try to determine:

- How long the person has been unconscious.

- The cause.

- If the person is breathing.

- If the person has a heartbeat.

- If the person has been ill. For how long?

- The person's medical history.

Complete the following actions:

- Lie the person flat on the floor.

- Do not put a pillow behind the person's head.

- Turn the person on one side, if vomiting or drooling.

- Perform mouth-to-mouth or CPR, if needed.

Allergic Reactions/Stings

In cases of allergic reactions or insect bites or stings, try to determine:

- If the person is breathing.

- If the person has a heartbeat.

- What caused the allergic reaction, if known (insect bite, commercial product, etc.).

- If the person has a history of allergies.
- If the person has any medication for allergies.
- If the person recently ate.
- If the person has recently been bitten or stung.
- If the person has recently taken or injected any medications.

Complete the following actions:

- Give mouth-to-mouth, if necessary.
- Give chest compressions (CPR), if necessary.
- If person is conscious, place in a comfortable position.

12

THE BIG DAY

En route to the picnic, they drive through their history, telling jokes and watching the road
— "PICNIC: THE LIBERATED" BY M. CARL HOLMAN

It's taken almost a year to plan, but now the big day is finally here. Maybe you're a little nervous, a little excited. Hopefully, you've had a good night's sleep. You're going to need it. Since you will be dividing your time between making sure everything goes smoothly and trying to enjoy some of the benefits of your own planning, you're going to need every ounce of energy you can muster.

TIPS FOR THE SINGLE-PERSON ORGANIZER

The night before my family reunions, I'm so excited, I find it difficult to get to sleep. I tend to agonize over last-minute details. I can't help but feel that there's something that I forgot to do. I stress over all of the things that could possibly go wrong.

The night before your reunion, if you find yourself in that state of sleepless panic, don't agonize—strategize! I find this exercise helpful to help ease my anxiety. To clear your mind of all of those "what ifs", write them down. Take out a pencil and paper and draw a line down the middle of the page. Or, if composing by computer is easier for you, create a two-column table. On the top of the left column, write "What if...." Label the top of the right column "Then I...."

Spend a few minutes listing all of your fears and answers to problems. For example, what if it rains? Then I use the rain day contingency plan. Or, what if the caterer doesn't arrive on time with the food? Then I stall for time until the caterer gets there. Or, then I rush down to the nearest deli or fast-food restaurant and see what they can provide on short notice. Or what if the disc jockey starts to play an inappropriate song? Then I ask the disc jockey to quickly put on another selection. Or I turn to the crowd and get them to shout out their favorites. Or I can start a sing-along or singing contest.

Don't turn the what if game into an all-night marathon. The purpose of this exercise is to reassure yourself of what, deep in your heart, you already know to be true: You've planned. You've prepared. You're ready. Facing down my worst nightmares before I go to sleep helps me to rest with greater peace of mind.

As you settle down for the night, don't forget to set your alarm. This is no time to oversleep. On the morning of your reunion, you want to be fresh, energetic, ready to face the day with anticipation. If your start the day off feeling like you're running late, you'll spend the rest of the day feeling like you're running behind. In my family, when someone is habitually late, we call it running on CP time. Make it stand for Conscientious Person's time or Committed Person's time.

TIPS FOR COMMITTEE-BASED PLANNERS: GO TEAM!

That's the spirit you want to invoke on the day before the reunion. If the single-person planner has fears and concerns the night before the reunion, the committee-based organizers will have those fears magnified by the number of people involved on your committee.

On the night before the picnic, call your committee members together. Spend a few minutes checking and double-checking that each committee person knows what they are supposed to be doing and when. Go through your individual checklists. If any members are nervous about oversleeping, appoint a person to give wake-up calls as a last resort.

After you complete the last bit of committee business, spend a few moments the night before reassuring one another that you have planned well. Give yourselves encouragement. You have done well. Your reunion will go smoothly because you have planned, because you are organized.

In Chapter 5, we reviewed the events that must be put into place to make this day happen. This chapter will apply those practical points and help you bring those plans to fruition.

The items to check include:

- Weather

- Location

- Activities

- Food

- Music

- Security

- Cleanup

WEATHER

The first thing to do once you wake us is to check the weather report. What does the news from the paper, television, or radio say about today? Sunny and hot? Dark and rainy? If you've been watching the news the week before the reunion, you have an idea of how the weather will be. But here is your chance to make one final check before plunging into the day's events. If the weather isn't going to cooperate, you have enough advance notice to put your contingency plan into place.

Proceed to the designated area and put up the rain-day contingency notices. If your contingency plan for bad weather is to hold the reunion at a church or community center, make certain to notify church officials or the community-center administrator of your change in plans. You'll want to have someone standing by to open the doors, put up any signs or notices, and freshen the area before your relatives arrive.

Contact the heads of each committee and make sure they notify those who will be providing a good or service, such as the caterer or deejay, of the change in plans.

If the weather promises to be perfect for your reunion, contact your helpers and get the day started.

LOCATION

If you're sure that the weather will cooperate, follow through with the plan to proceed to the picnic site. Contact the relatives who were selected to grab that perfect spot and make certain that they are in place. These early birds can use the time waiting for the arrival of other family members to set up balloons, banners, and signs; fire up the barbecue grill; set up the hospitality tents or tables; and perform whatever tasks necessary to get the family reunion started.

REGISTRATION

Thanks to the early birds, the signs and banners have all been put up and are now fluttering in the breeze. Their bright colors are designed to attract your family members like bees to honey. The deejay has the music playing. Your favorite songs are echoing across the picnic grounds, making you move and groove to the beat of your favorite tunes. The scrumptious smells are wafting through the air as the appointed chefs for the day are busy flipping those sizzling burgers on the grill.

By now, your family members will be arriving by the carloads. With so much going on around them, the temptation will be for your family members to jump right into the activities. You may have a few eager family members who want to eat right away or start the games now. If you are a single-person planner, part of your responsibility is to make sure that the reunion moves according to the schedule you have provided.

As your family members arrive, you want them to stop by the registration table to pick up their registration packets. Remember, registration time is the perfect opportunity to address any last-minute issues. Do you have the family member's correct address? Do you have a complete list of every family member? Has everyone paid their dues? This is also the time to thank your family members for coming out and to make them feel appreciated for sharing in this moment.

The greeters at the registration table, if they are friendly and persistent, will be able to get the last minute administrative details out of the way and have your relatives feeling like VIPs. Reinforce how happy you are to see them.

ACTIVITIES

A boring, disorganized, left-to-chance reunion can hamper your chances of a grand turnout for the next reunion. No matter how perfect the weather is or how delicious the food may be, a family reunion that allows boredom or confusion to creep in will not be remembered fondly. Planned activities give your reunion a sense of movement—of progress.

These events will only go like clockwork if you have a schedule. Having a clear idea of the events you will have at the reunion will also help you decide what items you need for activities to take place. For example, if you plan to have a water-balloon contest, the person or committee in charge of that event is responsible for making certain that there are adequate balloons, a source of water, such as a spigot and garden hose, and that the event starts on time.

Sample Schedule courtesy of Orlean Dorsey, Jackson Family Reunion, 1998.

PICNIC SCHEDULE
10:00 A.M. ARRIVAL

Time	Event	Person in Charge
11:30	Water-balloon competition	Raynard
12:00	Egg toss competition	
	Ages: 3–12, 13 and up	Doris
12:15	Let's Eat!	Frederick
2:00	Sack Races	
	Ages: 3–5, 6–10, 11–17, 18 and up	
2:30	Cards and Dominoes	
3:00	Volleyball competition	Rodney
3:30	Tug-of-war	Fred
4:00	Putting Competition	Raynard

Icebreakers

The first planned events should include an icebreaker, or something done or said to relax an unduly formal atmosphere or situation. Sometimes, family members who live close together or those who know one another well have a tendency to congregate in one area.

Other family members who are separated by distance or are new additions to the family may be a little shy about participating in the conversations of those close-knit groups. Keep an eye out for these loners. Remember that though you are all family, this may be the first time that some of you have laid eyes on one another. You want to make everyone feel welcome and involved.

If you are a single-person organizer, this is your opportunity to play cheerleader. You want to get the crowd stirred up. You want to get them off their feet, out of their seats, and into the mix. Be enthusiastic. But you must also be sympathetic. Sometimes, no matter how much you try, some family members will refuse to participate in the activities. Be sensitive to those who do not want to join in. For those who do, get ready for more than enough laughter and fun to fill the void.

Here are a few suggestion for "breaking up" the family while drawing you closer together.

Puzzle Put-Together

Include individual pieces from several puzzles in the family reunion invitations or registration packets. Include instructions on what the puzzle piece is for. Family members are supposed to find others with pieces that complete the puzzle. At the end of the reunion, the family members with the most complete puzzle win a prize.

As the reunion facilitator or the judge of the event, you'll have a lot less guesswork with trying to determine the winner if you purchase different puzzles with the same amount of puzzle pieces. If you have a large family and expect many family members to attend, complex puzzles offer the most opportunity for family members to interact. If you have a small family, smaller puzzles will be less frustrating for family members to try to put together. And don't forget the younger children. Puzzle pieces containing ten or fewer pieces are appropriate for family members eight years old and under.

Treasure Hunt

Hand out blank sheets of paper and pencils. Send people off in search of signatures from the oldest family member present, the person who traveled the farthest to attend, or the family with the most immediate members present. Let the family members be creative about gathering signatures. As they mix and mingle, they will discover interesting points about other family members, which will add to your family's unique heritage.

Family Tree

Line up people as their names would appear on a genealogical tree chart of the family tree. Take a picture from the young end first, then have everyone turn around and a take a picture of the group from the oldest end.

Birthday Game

Have all of the members of the family born in the same month stand together. See if you can locate family members born on the same day. Have a caller shouting out the months and indicating which areas are designated for which month. Encourage your family members to discuss their birth dates. You can generate more excitement for the game if your family members know what prizes they may win. Do any family members have the same birthday? Issue prizes. Are any relatives born on a special holiday? Issue more prizes.

I have several aunts and uncles who *never* admit to their true age. With a prize as an incentive to tell the year of their births, my cousins resort to all kinds of means to get the truth out of them, including bribery, sneaking peeks at their driver's licenses, even humorous threats of blackmail.

Toilet Tissue Game

This is a variation of a game I see often at baby showers. Pass around rolls of toilet tissue. Let each person tear off a few squares. When everyone has their squares, ask them to tell one thing about themselves for each square they've taken. You can give them a couple of freebie squares such as giving their names and where they are from.

For example, if your Aunt Mary has taken off five squares, she has to list five things about herself. As she lists something about herself, she can tear off a square. My name is Mary. I'm from Jackson, Mississippi. (Those are the two freebies). Then the person must be creative and tell something different and interesting about herself.

Family Auction

When you send out the invitations and notices, you can ask for donations to the family auction. As you bring out items of interest, or items recognized by your family members, you'll find that the excitement generated by Aunt so-and-so's faux pearl necklace will become contagious. The proceeds from the auction can be applied to the next reunion.

Hot Potato

Break up your family members into groups. Have the groups form circles. In the center of a circle, let someone stand with a small tennis ball and a bell or whistle. The facilitator tosses the ball to someone in the circle. That person tosses the ball to someone else. When the facilittor rings the bell or blows the whistle, the person left with the ball must tell three things about himself: Name, where they're from, and something different, such as a nickname or favorite hobby.

Simple Charades

Have your family members form circles. Each person gives his name and where he is are from. Then, the person gives a clue about something they will act out, such as a favorite hobby, television show, or what they do for a living.

Door Prizes

Pass out tickets or numbers to every member who attends the reunion. A volunteer, reaches into a bowl or sack holding the duplicates of those numbers. When your number is called, you win a prize.

For a one-day picnic, you will only need one or two icebreakers in order to get your relatives primed for fun. Once they get into the spirit of the reunion, continue with the rest of your scheduled activities. Make sure to keep a mix of high-energy and low-impact games. High-energy games for the young and young-at-heart, such as soccer, softball, and flag football give your family members a chance to play at being a weekend warrior. Low impact games, such as checkers, dominoes, or photo identification contests (see page 158) appeal to the less physically active.

The following are a few more reunion activities to help fill the day with the reunion memories to last a lifetime.

High-Energy Games

Friendly Competition Games

Games such as sack races, tug-of-war, egg toss, or volleyball can certainly go a long way toward breaking the ice. Pit one family against another, girls against boys, young against old. Any combination will work wonders for getting your family members out of their seats.

You can play standard favorites like softball or football. But to avoid doing the "same old thing" every year, try to put a twist on the games. For example, in softball, if you make it on to base, you have to give an interesting fact about yourself. The more times you get on base, the more people will learn about you. If you strike out, you have to stand up and recite your favorite poem, Bible verse, or song. This may extend the length of the game, but it helps your family members to get to know one another.

Inflatable Tent

A large, inflatable tent where children can bounce and somersault is a big hit at family reunion picnics.

Push the Peanut/Roll the Egg

Place your family members in a long line side by side. Place a peanut or boiled egg in front of them. The family members must push the object to the finish line with their noses.

Low-Impact Activities

Photo Contest

Place baby photos of your relatives and a number next to each one on a huge bulletin board or corkboard. Pass out sheets of paper, and let everyone try to guess who is in the picture.

Family History Table

Set up a long table with photographs and artifacts unique to your family. A handmade quilt lovingly crafted by your great-grandmother, the dog tags from your uncle's stint in the army, pictures of the first family members to arrive in your state, invitations from the last cousin to graduate, all make wonderful conversation topic pieces.

Family Sing-along

Sing songs that stress the importance of family togetherness and reliance on one another. At a family reunion that I once attended, the song, "Family Reunion" by the O'Jays was popular. "Lean on Me" by Bill Withers was also a reunion favorite.

Other Activities:

- Silly contests such as bubble-gum blowing, watermelon-seed spitting.

- Name That Tune, in which the deejay plays a few seconds from a song. Form different teams to guess the name of the song.

FOOD

You or your planning teams have already decided on the types of meals that will be served at the picnic. Is everyone going to bring their own food or is it going to be catered? If catered, make a final call to the caterer to verify that they have the time and location of the event.

If everyone is going to bring their own, keep in mind that certain foods will spoil faster than others if not refrigerated. Potato or pasta salads are notorious for "going bad" if left too long in the sun. Keep ice chests for any family member who needs a little extra ice to keep foods safe.

MUSIC

Your deejay should be at the picnic site no later than one hour before the scheduled reunion time. You want him to have time to set up and test the equipment one final time before your family starts to arrive. This allows you time to adjust the loudness of the music without annoying your relatives with bursts of speaker static or microphone feedback. With the music already playing when they arrive, it is a lure and an additional welcome for them.

SECURITY

Have your security at the reunion site at the crack of dawn with your early birds. They need watching over, as well. During the course of the day, make sure that the security is patrolling the full area of your picnic. Though you want the officer to be friendly, you don't want someone who is *too* friendly. If you see the security officer spending too much time in one location, politely but firmly request for him to circulate more.

CLEANUP

At my family reunion, when it looks as if time is winding down, the children will usually scatter. They know what's coming. Any child who happens to be near an adult when someone says "Time to clean up!" can guarantee that he will be part of the cleanup force. A fun way of getting children involved with cleaning up is to have a contest. The child with the most completely filled garbage bags wins an award. Just be careful as your junior cleanup crew starts collecting materials that they aren't premature in their collection.

I've attended several Jackson Family Reunions hosted by the relatives of Mary Livingston. And on each occasion, the dismayed cries of relatives who stepped away only to find their unfinished plates of food or soda cans prematurely whisked away resounded through the entire event.

REMEMBRANCES OF REUNIONS PAST
MARY JANE DUNCAN LIVINGSTON,
JACKSON FAMILY REUNION, 1996

We like to have our family reunions in wide, open spaces. That way, we can spread out, and all of the younger children can run and play and scream as much as they like without bothering anyone. As far as games, we always have a volleyball tournament. For years, when we had the family reunions at our homestead site in LaGrange, Texas, it was always the Houston Jacksons against the LaGrange Jacksons. The LaGrange team would talk a lot of noise, saying how living in the city made us soft. We'd tease them back saying how living in the country had made them slow. We would get the little ones, who are too small to play with the grownups involved, too. One year, we had special T-shirts made just for the little kids. They were our cheerleaders. They stood on the sidelines and cheered for their mamas and daddies in the game. When the LaGrange Jacksons whipped our tails in volleyball (after we laughingly accused them of cheating), we vowed we would get them next year. Knowing that they're waiting for us makes it fun to go back year after year.

13

THE MULTIDAY EVENT

Luck is what happens when preparation
meets opportunity.

—AUTHOR UNKNOWN

Hosting a reunion that spans several days offers more challenges than a single-day event, such as a picnic. To organize a reunion on a larger scale, you take the effort of planning a one-day event and apply that same level of intensity, activity, commitment, and enthusiasm over an entire weekend.

However, planning a multiday event offers its share of rewards, as well. One benefit of hosting a multiday reunion is the increased opportunity for sharing ourselves with our relatives. Sometimes, when we are in the middle of our family reunions, time passes so quickly, that before we know it, the day is gone. This is especially true for single-day events. As planners, there is so much to do and so many people that attend the reunion, that we may not get around to hugging everyone or learning every name.

Planning a multiday event gives you a chance to pace yourself. With the proper balance of planning, participation, and peace and quiet, you can divide your time between

128

planning the events and getting acquainted with your family members. After all, they are the reason for this occasion.

TIPS FOR THE SINGLE-PERSON ORGANIZER

During a multiday reunion, the single-person organizer may sometimes feel more like an athlete than an active member of the family. Remember, the single-person organizer is the main contact for all of the activities planned during a multiday event. Although the single-person organizer may have friends and other relatives who have volunteered their knowledge and services to make sure everything runs smoothly, if things do not, the single-person organizer is going to be the "go to" person. *You* are the problem solver, the way maker. You will be expected to know the answers.

If you have kept a firm handle on every detail while planning the reunion, you will be able to handle most problems quickly and easily. Sometimes situations crop up that are beyond your control and beyond your knowledge. Even if you don't know the answer immediately, pretend that you do. There is an old saying—fake it until you make it. Buy yourself a little time. When your "helpers" come to you with issues, be calm, be patient. They will be looking to you to help them resolve the problems they could not. Solving problems quickly, effectively, and with a sense of humor is what makes you an effective leader.

TIPS FOR COMMITTEE-BASED REUNIONS

When planning a multiday event by committee, communication and coordination are critical to hosting a successful reunion. You've likely spent a year or more planning this event. If, for any reason, you must deviate from any part of the plan, make sure that all of the committee members know the new one. This will prevent passing on wrong information to your relatives. For example, you don't want anyone left out of the group picture because the time or location changed at the last minute and the committee planning this event did not communicate the change.

One way to make certain that events go smoothly is to have regular check-in meetings by the heads of the committees. It doesn't have to be a formal meeting—a quick, ten to fifteen minute meeting at a designated time and place. Some committees meet once in the morning, once around lunchtime, and once in the evening.

Go over the agenda for the day and confirm that everyone knows what they are supposed to be doing. For example, for the team handling the children's games, have all the games been purchased? Have the games been delivered to the right location? Who will set up the games? Who will coordinate the games? Who will see that the equipment is picked up and returned once the picnic is over?

Even with careful planning, there are many unforeseen eventualities that may cause you to grit your teeth. Turn the unfortunate incidents into golden opportunities. Don't grit your teeth. Grin and bear it.

REMEMBRANCES OF REUNIONS PAST
VALERIE MERLETT, SIMMONS FAMILY REUNION, 1997

We had planned all of these wonderful activities for our family reunion. We had enough outdoor activities to please everyone, three-legged sack races, water-balloon fights, volleyball. And then it started to rain. Buckets and buckets. It didn't seem like it would ever let up. We moved everyone inside to get out of the downpour. We had to think fast to come up with something for all of those people to do.

We went into a local sporting-goods store, dripping wet but still proudly wearing our reunion T-shirts. When the manager saw us all wearing our T-shirts, he volunteered to help us out with our reunion. He offered us items from his store free of charge! Coloring books and crayons for the kids, paddleballs, items like that. That gave us ideas for the next reunion. You never know what you can get until you ask. That manager really made our reunion.

ORGANIZING THE WEEKEND

Reunions that span an entire weekend are usually broken up into four main segments. The first part of this chapter will give you an overview of some of the events that may occur during the course of your weekend reunion. The second part of the chapter gives you some ideas on how to put the pieces in place that will make for a reunion that will be remembered for years to come.

Friday Night

Friday is the usually kickoff night for a weekend reunion. This is the time that most of your relatives will be arriving from out of town. Maybe some only had a short distance to travel. Maybe some have been on the road for a couple of days. The first thing they should see when they arrive at the hotel is the friendly, smiling faces of the hospitality committee. The hospitality committee is responsible for making relatives feel welcome. They reduce the anxiety of being among strangers.

Registration Desk

To be certain that your relatives do feel welcome when they arrive, set up the family reunion registration desk the night before, if possible, to be available to early arrivals. The registration desk should be clearly marked with banners with your family name or balloons. Centerpieces, such as floral arrangements, are attractive. Yet, they may also take up valuable space on the table. This is where your relatives will be signing names, filling out forms, and picking up their packets. Keep a good supply of pencils or pens handy. The easier it is for your family members to pick up their reunion information, the faster you can see to the needs of the next relative.

Keep in mind that as relatives congregate around the table, they will want to greet one another and perform a mini "long time, no see" reunion on the spot. This sight is encouraging to the hospitality team to see so much goodwill happening right before their eyes. But it may be somewhat discouraging for those waiting in line to pick up their reunion information. After a long trip, your relatives will want to get to their rooms as soon as possible before jumping into the reunion festivities. Encourage your family members to catch up at the night's hospitality event. If there is a line of waiting relatives, keep the line moving as briskly as possible. Be sensitive to the needs of all—the welcomed and the weary.

The registration desk should contain the list of all of the family members who have preregistered. As the family members arrive, check off their names and pass out their family reunion registration packets.

The registration desk should also contain blank registration forms for any last-minute guests. You want to make everyone feel welcome. Now is the time to verify the names, addresses, and personal information of your family members. This final, composite list will be what you use to mail out any follow-up information about the reunion, keepsakes, or mementos.

Registration packets

Keep the registration packets at the desk. These packets contain all the reunion information your family members will need:

- Agenda or schedule

- Materials from tourism boards

- Donations from corporations

- Keepsakes such as T-shirts or hats

- Maps to the picnic site or banquet

- Name tags

- Meal tickets

- Family update form

You may also want to include a list of committee contacts.

Everyone who has preregistered should have an envelope or a bag labeled with their name. Manila envelopes in nine by twelve or ten by thirteen sizes are usually large enough to hold all of the reunion materials. The envelopes can be purchased at general-merchandise stores or office-supply stores. Manila or white envelopes are the least expensive; but colored envelopes add a splash of pizzazz.

If your family reunion has a special theme or logo, a little preparation will add a special touch to the reunion packets. Use a computer and scanner to create a family logo. Chapter 7 describes the tools and methods for creating this type of artwork. Once you have the perfect design, you can use a photocopier to copy that logo onto the blank envelopes or create special labels to apply to the envelopes.

Or, if corporate sponsors and tourism bureaus have been especially generous with freebies, you can use plastic bags to hold your reunion materials. Plastic bags with handles can be purchased at party-supply stores.

Keep separate boxes of the registration packets at the registration desk. In one box, keep the packets of the family members who have preregistered. To make the packets easier to find, keep them in alphabetical order. Or, you can keep the packets together by family.

In another box, keep packets for the relatives or guests who did not preregister. This may seem awkward or slightly embarrassing for the relatives who did not preregister for the reunion. Use this as an opportunity to make that relative or guest feel especially welcome. There may be many reasons why this family did not send in their dues. Perhaps this relative recently learned of the family reunion. Perhaps, their payment was lost or never received.

As the single-person organizer, this is your opportunity to put on the hat of the diplomat. If the relative's name is not on the list and the relative insists that the funds were sent, you must be gracious and patient. Apologize for the oversight and issue that relative a registration packet. Later, you can put on the hat of the detective to determine the location of the missing funds.

Hospitality Night/Get-Acquainted Dinner

Fridays are also reserved for informal get-togethers. After your family members check in, they can relax and mingle with other relatives who have arrived. The hotel provides good locations, such as a banquet hall or conference room to interact. You can have the meal catered or, to save money, you can allow family members to bring their favorite dishes. Make sure that family members know that this get-acquainted night is informal. They may opt to skip this part of the reunion in order to rest from travel.

REMEMBRANCES OF REUNIONS PAST
MARY LIVINGSTON, JACKSON FAMILY REUNION, 1997

On Friday nights, we like to have a fish fry. Nothing formal. Just paper plates and cups, maybe a salad, and some french fries. Under the pavillion, we keep a couple of huge coolers with punch or water and condiments like tartar sauce and ketchup. It makes it easy because everyone can just serve themselves. It's kind of hard on the ones who have to cook, standing over that hot fry cooker to make sure that the fish doesn't burn. That's why we try to have the cookout late in the evenings. But we try to take turns so we can all enjoy the food and the family. Sometimes, we can't cook that fish fast enough. Something about being in the open air makes us extra hungry. We have to remind the little kids to wait, to let the fish cool, before they go digging in.

SATURDAY MORNING/AFTERNOON

For multiday reunions, by Saturday most of the family members who will be attending the reunion will have arrived. Because this day contains the largest amount of relatives, you will want to plan your events to accommodate the increased number of people.

Saturday morning and afternoons usually consists of a picnic. Chapter 12 provides some detailed activities that will help make your picnic reunion one to remember.

Even though maps were included with the registration packets, make certain that each family member has a ride to the picnic. If they do not, have them meet at a designated place, such as the hotel registration desk or the family reunion hospitality desk.

The transportation committee coordinates rides to and from the picnic. Use a checklist or tally sheet to keep an accurate account of who rode with whom. Write down their passengers' names. Make sure they know what time drivers will be coming back to the hotel. Passengers must meet you at the appointed site and time even if they intend to catch a ride back with someone else. Indicate on the checklist the family members who did not come back with you and why. If they do not come back with you, have them initial the space next to their names.

SATURDAY EVENING

Formal affairs, such as banquets, are reserved for Saturday evenings. A formal sit-down dinner gives your family the opportunity to dress up in their finery to put their best face forward. Remember, they have just spent an afternoon, running, screaming, and generally playing havoc with their appearance. A formal sit-down dinner gives your family more time to catch up with long-lost relatives in a less hectic atmosphere.

This doesn't mean solemn or boring. A popular activity to hold at a reunion is a roast, where family members tell amusing stories about one another.

Banquet nights are also opportunities for family members to showcase their unique talents.

SUNDAY MORNING

First giving honor and glory to God...

As part of my Sunday-morning church services, each time a member stood to speak or give a testimony, we prefaced our speech with that solemn phrase. My family's spirituality is deeply rooted. Our faith sustained us when we had little else to keep us going. Family reunions are a time to celebrate the bountiful blessings of kinship and family.

Sunday-morning worship services allows us to thank God for bringing us together one more year. We also pray for safe passage as we break for home.

Leaving enough time open between events gives family members the downtime they need to take a break. Remember, many of your family members have traveled a distance to participate in the family reunion. Scheduling time to rest means they can attend the reunion with enough energy and enthusiasm.

14

PRESERVING THE TRADITIONS/PASSING THE TORCH

Her eyes were gentle; her voice was for soft singing
In the stiff-backed pew, or on the front porch when
evening comes slowly over Atlanta. But she
remembered.
—"AN OLD WOMAN REMEMBERS" BY STERLING A BROWN

*W*ho wants to hear about that old-timey, slavery day stuff?

At some family reunions, it's the rallying cry for the younger generation. When older aunts and uncles at my family reunions come together to discuss the stories of long ago, my younger cousins scatter as fast as their youthful legs can carry them. Unable or unwilling to make the connection between what happened thirty, forty, or fifty years ago, and how it affects their lives today, the younger members of family seek refuge from those "boring stories."

I know why I used to run when I was younger. My family sometimes used those shared experience of trials and triumphs to gloat over the younger ones—reminding us with every word how they sacrificed for us *ungrateful* kids.

Instead of holding out our strength, our tenacity, our family pride as a baton, using it to lead the way, we use those stories as a club, beating it over the heads of our youth. We brand them with terms like "Generation X" giving them an undefined place in the family chain. We frown at their loud music, their odd style of dressing, their language.

As a reunion organizer, if you never plan another picnic, break bread at another banquet, or mail out another memento, you must bridge the gap between young and old.

You must ensure that everyone in the family recognizes and respects the importance of their role and their place in the family line. Young and old—each has a role to play in preserving the family history and guaranteeing its future.

We depend on our youth to be our beacons of the future. "Each child is an adventure into a better life—an opportunity to change the old pattern and make it new." Our language is filled with phrases that tell us how important our children are to us. "A mind is a terrible thing to waste" or "It takes a whole village to raise a child" are such examples.

PRESERVING HISTORY

As the single-person organizer, here is your chance to play the part of investigative reporter. An investigative reporter does more than report simple facts, such as where and when an event occurred. He digs deeper to get to the heart of the story. To preserve your family's history, you want to know more than just when and where a relative was born. You want to know what that relative was really like.

When researching my family genealogy, I learned that my grandmother grew up during the Great Depression. In school, I'd studied history books that explained the Stock Market crash of 1929. I read how many Americans became bankrupt overnight, some preferring to commit suicide rather than face financial ruin. I've studied economics textbooks presenting a variety of theories to explain business cycles, booms, and recessions. But none of those books made a lasting impact on me until I learned from my grandmother what it mean to be a child during the Depression era.

Even as a child, my grandmother worked long hours for pennies a day scrubbing floors to help put food on the table for her sisters and brothers. Because food was a constant concern in her family, to this day, she always ensures that she has prepared enough for everyone to have plenty. When she shops, she compares prices—always looking for the bargains that will make her dollars stretch farther. She is both generous and frugal.

She once told me the story of how she had to strip the wax from floors using gasoline and a scrub brush. At the end of the day, her payment was forty cents—a dime per floor! Knowing that my grandmother, a woman dear to my heart, worked for forty cents for a full-day's work means so much more to me than what history dispassionately calls "a period in an industrial nation characterized by low production and sales and a high rate of business failures and unemployment."

My grandmother tells these stories not to make her family feel guilty for our modern conveniences, but to encourage us to strive for a better life for our children.

Oral History

The practice of passing along family history through word of mouth is not unique to my family. This ancient practice comes to all of us from our African ancestors. In African villages, a griot (*GREE-oh*) is responsible for keeping the history of the village alive through tales and songs. Often, that history includes several generations.

Anyone who has seen the dramatization of Alex Haley's *Roots* may remember the final scene when actor James Earl Jones, portraying Alex Haley, discovers the birthplace of his forefather Kunta Kinte through a village griot. The griot described all of the generations of that village to finally connect Haley to that time and place through his forefather's name.

When Africans were brought to America, through indentured servitude or as unwilling slaves, the tradition of preserving oral history was continued. Because it was illegal to teach slaves to read or write, the spoken word was one way they could preserve the memories of their land, their families, their culture.

Written History

My grandmother keeps a family Bible. In this Bible, she records the names and birthdays of her children, her children's children, and so on. It's a large Bible. And over the years and frequent use, it's become cracked and faded. The pages are filled with so many names, you can barely find space in the Bible to add another. When I flip through the pages, I find cousins that I was unaware that I had. It reminds me that there is still so much I don't know about my own family.

Maybe your family has a similar method of keeping track of your family's progress. However, your family's history is more than just a collection of births and deaths. Think of your family history as a narrative, a tale that changes from person to person and from moment to moment. Sometimes the tale may feel like a tragedy, full of heartaches and disappointments. Sometimes your family's tale may read like a comedy, complete with the consummate jokesters who kept up sagging spirits during trying times. Maybe your family's history reads like an action-adventure story, with brave, unsung heroes who risked their lives to see that others in the family succeeded. A simple list of names and dates is important to keeping us connected to individual family members, but it does not do justice to the individual accomplishments.

COLLECTING YOUR FAMILY HISTORY

Use the family reunion to begin collecting your family's history. With everyone gathered for a family reunion, you get more than one perspective on the events that shaped your family. Once you get your family members talking, you may find that no two individuals will remember an event in exactly the same way. Maybe one family member remembers a specific event as happening in the summer of 1942. Another relative might recall the same event as occurring in the spring of 1943. Don't get discouraged when you come across these kinds of discrepancies. The important thing is to get the flavor of the moment. What was the event? How were your relatives involved? How did it make them feel?

Collect the Facts

The first step toward collecting your family's history is to gather the facts. Facts include the pieces of information similar to what's recorded in my family Bible. When were you born? Who are your siblings? What are their names and birth dates. Who are your parents? When were they born, and so on. Start with yourself and go back as far as you can.

Because there is so much going on at a family reunion, you may want to begin collecting facts before the reunion actually begins. While you are researching the names and addresses of family members or gathering recipes for the family cookbook, you can also begin to build your family tree. Make each family responsible for listing themselves, their children, and their children's children. Encourage them to list their parents and their parents' parents, going back as far as they can.

Use all sources of information to collect family-history facts. Birth certificates, family Bibles, old letters, even birthday cards can help you build the outline around the story you will develop at the family reunion.

Later I give some tips and tools that will help you on your family's fact-finding mission.

Preparing to Research

It takes time, patience, and persistence to become the family historian and genealogist. The sooner you begin your research, the more useful information you can find. Like an investigative reporter, you must begin your research with a goal in mind. For example, how far back do you want to try to trace your family? How many branches of your family do you want to investigate?

If you have a large family with many branches, it may not be possible to present all information at one reunion. Some families focus their reunions on one branch of the family at a time.

Once you have a clear idea of how far you want to go, then gather materials that will help you in your search. As you gather each item, include it on a checklist so that when you are ready to begin your research, you will leave nothing behind, nothing to chance. Here are a few items that may be included on your checklist. These items will be useful whether you are hunting through the halls of a genealogy library or wading through the weeds in a long-forgotten cemetery.

Back to Basics

● Pencils, paper, and highlighters. Like going to school, it is almost impossible to begin a family research venture without these basic elements. I use different highlighters to indicate to which branch of the family a relative belongs. I keep all of my notes in a three-ring binder. As you discover a family member, place a checkmark in the corner of that page once you determine to which branch of the family that relative belongs. Later, you can reshuffle the pages to keep like "colors" together. This will help you sort out family members when you begin to present your family-history memento.

- Longsleeves, long pants, thick-soled shoes. When researching your family history, it may be necessary to tread on long-forgotten paths in long-forgotten cemeteries. Protect yourself from overgrown weeds, briars, and even insect bites with insect repellent. When selecting your shoes, make sure that they are comfortable. You don't want to kill the spirit of adventure and discovery with complaints of aching, blistered feet.

Mechanical Advantages

These items may come in handy during your search:

- Tape recorder with power adapter and extra batteries. In face-to-face interviews, sometimes your fingers will not be able to transcribe as fast as the relatives giving you their accounts of your life history. The tape recorder will help you capture the flavor of the moment.

- Camera with additional rolls of film and batteries. Chapter 10 discusses types of cameras and the benefits of each type. The more advanced the camera, the longer the life of the photograph. If you will be using a camera to take pictures of documents, such as birth certificates or other vital records, digital cameras are more expensive, but they offer features that will help capture more information.

- Laptop computer, AC adapter, additional batteries. A laptop computer provides a portable means of accessing, storing, and changing vast amounts of information quickly and easily.

- Hardware options or additions, such as PC cards; fax modems; CD-ROM, floppy, or Zip drives means that you can make volumes of information such as telephone directories of various cities, ready for travel.

RESEARCHING AT THE REUNION

Some family members use the actual reunion as the start of their reunion research. If you want to start building the family tree at the reunion, you may locate two or three individuals who have the most knowledge of the family. But since this is a family-oriented occasion, try to get everyone's participation.

"One year, we put up a giant poster on a wall of the banquet room. It covered almost an entire wall. We had lots of Magic Markers available. At the top of the paper, we put the name of our great-grandparents. Then, we listed the names of their children. After that, everyone was invited to come up and write their names on the poster where they fit into the family," remembers Orlean Dorsey, organizer of the Jackson Family Reunion.

If you're a single-person organizer, it may be difficult for you to be around to hear all of the conversations about your family's past. One way to make sure you gather as much information as you can is to have roving reporters canvassing the reunion. Give them video cameras or tape recorders. Make sure you have plenty of charged batteries for both, to encourage movement, or a power source if you intend to stay in one place. You will also need several blank cassettes for tape recorders or camcorders. Leave unused cassettes or batteries in their original packaging until you are ready to use them. Unused items can all be returned for a refund if you have the receipt.

You can also set up a "Memory Lane" booth. Place a couple of comfortable chairs in a quiet, out-of-the-way spot. Set up a camcorder on a tripod or have a family member shoot in order to catch different angles. Invite family members to come by and give one story about what it was like growing up.

Some family members may be a little camera shy. Or, they may believe that nothing interesting has happened in their lives. Ensure them that their experiences are valuable. Don't ask them open-ended questions such as, "what were you like as a child." Ask specific questions such as, "Tell me about your first day of school." Or "Tell me what happened on your sixteenth birthday." "When was the first time you laid eyes on your husband or wife?"

Questions like these evoke both factual dates and emotions. It will not be possible to cover a person's entire life in an hour. Sometimes, interviews may go on for hours. Keep a notebook on hand to record extra notes in the event that your batteries become drained. Once the reunion is over, you can create a video documentary of the event.

REUNION PROGRAM BOOK

A family reunion keepsake book provides some treasured reminders of the time you have spent together with your loved ones. When you will distribute these reunion books determines the information that will go in them.

For example, if you plan to distribute them before or during the reunion, you may include information such as family history and poems. But, if you plan to distribute the keepsakes after the reunion, in a mailing, you can include photographs of the reunion.

Creating the Reunion Book

Copy

Creating a family reunion program book is similar to creating a family newsletter. You have copy. This is the information that makes up the body of the reunion book. The copy should be interesting to read and free of spelling errors. To make sure that you present the information in the best possible light, have several people read the copy before you compile it into the final format. If you are in contact with the family members responsible for putting out the family newsletter, they can be a valuable resource in helping you refine your program book.

Graphics, such as photographs, drawings, or clip art are also a nice touch to a reunion book. Be careful not to have too many. You want your reunion book to be visually appealing.

Cover

The cover of your family reunion book must be especially attractive. Because this book represents you and your family, it will be a source of pride for you all. The cover should include a family theme or motto, if you have one, and the date and location of the family reunion.

Content

Most reunion books include a special letter or note from the reunion chairperson or organizer.

15

WRAPPING UP

There is no end
To the shocks of morning.
—"SUMMER ORACLE" BY AUDRE LORDE

Sticker shock. I heard that phrase on a car commercial. It was a jazzy commercial, showing a sleek car that skimmed the road like a rocket, it took blind corners effortlessly, and left the lesser-equipped cars in the dust with its ability to accelerate. Then the price of the car was flashed along with fine print of what you needed to do to get this car. To poke fun at these commercial, economy-car commercials, use similar techniques. However, when the potential buyer comes to look at the sticker price, it literally makes their hair stand on end. Sticker shock.

It's what I call the expression on our faces when we finally get the bills for remaining reunion expenses, though, it shouldn't be *that* much of a shock. You should already have a pretty good idea of how much this reunion cost.

Take a look back at some of the previous chapters. They discussed some ideas for how to shop around for the best prices. One chapter showed how to make a budget. You've also been given a few ideas on holding fund-raisers to cover these costs. So, why does paying off the final bill cause such cries of dismay?

What price do you put on the experiences of a lifetime? Multiply that by the number of people you've touched and who have touched *you* during your family reunion. To adequately cover the cost of such priceless moments, as my daughter would say, it would cost a *gazillion* bucks!

Think of a family reunion as having an extra holiday. We may moan and groan about the overcrowded shopping malls, the commercialism, and the prices, but when it comes to seeing the joy on our family's faces, do we remember that aggravation? What stays with us long after we've paid off the bills is that, for a time, we brought joy to someone's life.

During your family reunion, you shared in the love and the laughter, met a relative, made a friend. You have gained some experiences, which turn into memories. Precious memories. When I think about it that way, it doesn't seem like a huge price to pay.

PAYING THE BILLS

After your reunion is over, there are usually miscellaneous bills and expenses that must be cleared. Paying these expenses promptly, and in full, generates goodwill between you and the parties involved. Building a good relationship now can only increase your bargaining power when it comes to planning and negotiating prices for the next reunion.

As the reunion organizer, you are responsible for making sure that everyone pays their bills as well. The most obvious expense that must be cleared after the reunion is over is the hotel bill. Relatives who rented rooms will clear their individual bills when they check out.

You will be responsible for paying the bills for items or services that everyone enjoyed, such as the banquet hall. When you close out the hotel bill, use that as an opportunity to collect specific information about how many rooms were actually rented, the number of meals that were served (including room service) and other hotel amenities. This information will be useful to you when creating a knowledge base for planning the next reunion.

Mary Livingston, an organizer of the Jackson Family Reunion advises, "We try to use the same motel for each of our reunions. They know us [and] we're such good repeat business. We're a rowdy bunch but we keep the noise down. We make sure to clean up after ourselves. Every year we use the same motel, we try to get more and more breaks from them, like free rooms."

RETURNING ITEMS

Part of the wrap-up process involves seeing that items that were rented or borrowed are returned. If you rented an inflatable tent for a day, the company supplying the tent is usually responsible for the setup, breakdown, and return of that item.

For other rented items, such as ice-makers, video equipment, or trash receptacles, it is your responsibility to see that they are returned to the rental offices on time and in good condition in order to get your deposit back. If you are late, there is usually a penalty, which varies depending on how late you are in returning the item. Some rented items, such as cars, will allow you to drop off the item at an alternate location. There may be a processing fee for the convenience of returning the item elsewhere.

When preparing to return items, make sure you leave enough time to break down the equipment, take inventory all of the pieces, and return to the rental store.

Items that are borrowed from friends or family members should be returned promptly and in good condition. One way to make certain that items get back to their rightful owners is to keep an inventory of borrowed items. Clearly describe the item such as: "one crystal punch bowl, slight chip near the base. Belongs to Cousin Mary Livingston." Note on the checklist when the item was returned and in what condition.

If the unthinkable happens and a borrowed item is damaged, be forthright about the damage and offer to replace or repair the damaged item.

CLEANING THE AREA

As you prepare to end your reunion, you will be remembered fondly by the hotel staff, community-center administrators, or park custodians if you are conscientious about removing all evidence of your event. This includes taking down all signs, banners, and balloons; removing all vestiges of tape or thumbtacks; and making sure the area isn't littered with your flyers or schedules.

16

IMPROVING ON A GRAND PLAN

Where are we to go when this is done?
Will we slip into old, accustomed ways?
—"SONNET" BY ALFRED A DUCKETT

*W*here does the time go? It's a question often asked of both reunion organizers and participants after the family reunion is over. You've spent a year planning for this event, and too soon, it's over—almost!

In a flurry of kisses and hugs, love and laughter, after exchanging names and numbers with promises to stay in touch, the last of the reunion attendees prepare to leave you behind. As the reunion organizer, that doesn't mean your job is done. In fact, when your relatives are leaving, you've got to switch into another gear. Some say that this is the point where work for the next reunion begins.

When people are packing up and preparing to leave, now is the perfect time to think about the next reunion. Undoubtedly you're brimming with ideas.

While everyone is feeling warm and receptive, take the time to reflect and review the areas of your family reunion that could have been better. Maybe one of your scheduled events didn't go over very well. Maybe the selection of food wasn't as varied as you'd wanted. Maybe you didn't get quite the turnout you were expecting. What would you like to have more of? What would you like to have less of? Now is the time to evaluate things. It's time to start thinking about how to duplicate your success and how to prevent your failures.

One way to organize those thoughts is to have a postmortem. A postmortem lets you review every phase, every aspect of the family reunion. As with the brainstorming session, the postmortem is not to point fingers and heap blame on what went wrong. The postmortem is meant to analyze the entire reunion, from beginning to end, and decide what worked well for your family reunion and what did not.

If you are planning by committee, set aside some time in your busy schedule to discuss all that you have accomplished so far. Discuss what you would like to accomplish at future reunions. Keep the meeting upbeat and positive. You can appoint a secretary or note taker to record ideas, or you can set up a tape recorder to capture the wealth of ideas that will come from this wrap-up session. With ideas flying back and forth so fast and furious, it will be difficult to take accurate notes without slowing down the creative process. You can always go back later and write down the concrete ideas that came out of this session.

PREPARING FOR FUTURE REUNIONS

The end of your family reunion is also the time to select the reunion organizers for next year. Sometimes this year's reunion organizers will be the same ones who will plan the next event. Sometimes that duty will pass on to another individual or another branch of the family.

When you orchestrate a successful reunion, there will be plenty of family members who will want to add their voices, to become a part of such a rewarding event.

Even if your family reunion did not go as well as planned, or if it hits a sour note, those family members who are convinced they can "do it better" will want to add their voices to the next planning session, as well. Before everyone scatters to go in their separate directions, make sure to communicate the date, time, and location of the next family reunion planning meeting. Nothing gets a good meeting off the ground like a challenge to make something better!

Make sure that everyone involved with planning this year's reunion is made known to the ones planning the next. The experiences of the current reunion planners are invaluable. They must be willing and eager to share their information in order to avoid making some of the same mistakes. Reunions can only get better if there is a sharing of duties, responsibilities, and credit for a job well done.

At some family reunions, the passing of information is not left to chance but made into a scheduled, formal event. Before everyone heads in their separate directions, a family meeting is held. With the entire family as witnesses, family members are chosen to hold certain positions, such as chairman of the site committee. These individuals are made responsible for completing the various planning tasks. It is a very serious, solemn occasion when they take on the task of preparing the next reunion. They publicly make a commitment to and for the family.

EVALUATION FORMS

Sometimes, it will not be possible to get feedback from your family members in a single meeting. As the reunion draws to a close, vacation time is winding down, and family members hurry off to catch their planes, there is little time for thinking about an event that may be a year or two away.

However, you would still like to get feedback on how the family felt about the reunion. An evaluation form is one means of collecting that type of information. You can distribute the evaluation forms as part of the reunion registration packet. Ask to have the forms returned before the reunion is over. Create a decorated box for the forms and place the box on the hospitality table. The advantage of passing out the forms at the reunion is that the feelings and impressions are fresh. Also, you have made the form easy to return, without having to worry about envelopes or postage.

Or, you can mail the evauation forms after the reunion in a follow-up questionnaire. If you are planning to mail your reunion keepsakes after the reunion, enclose the evaluation form. By packaging the form with the keepsakes and mementos, you may stir up fond memories of the reunion. However, a disadvantage to mailing your reunion evaluation form is that you may not get as high a return.

Sample Evaluation Form

The following is a sample family reunion survey form. Whether you intend to enclose the forms in the registration packets or mail them out after the reunion, be sure to include when, where, and how to return the form.

FAMILY NAME, YEAR
FAMILY REUNION FEEDBACK FORM

Now that our family reunion is done,
We hoped that you had tons of fun.
Making it better is our aim,
So take a few minutes to explain.
It's strictly confidential, so don't be shy—
What did you like—tell us why.
If something could be better, we want to know,
So next time we can improve the show!

Tell us about yourself:

What is your sex?　　Male＿＿＿　　　Female＿＿＿

How old are you? ＿＿＿

Present Reunion

On a scale of 1–4

1–excellent　　2–good　　3–fair　　4–poor

How would you rate:

The reunion location?
1　　2　　3　　4

The hotel accommodations?
1　　2　　3　　4

The meals?
1　　2　　3　　4

The planned activities?
1　　2　　3　　.4

The mementos?
1　　2　　3　　4

The reunion organizers/event coordinators?
1　　2　　3　　4

What did you like most about the reunion?

What did you like least?

Future Reunions

Give us some suggestions for the next reunion.

Would you attend? Tell us why or why not.

CONCLUSION

Now you can take a deep breath! Take a moment to sit back and reflect on the enormous task you've just completed. Look at all of the people, props, and events you've coordinated. It took months in the making, but the effort was well worth it. You've come away with renewed enthusiasm for keeping in touch with your loved ones. You've re-energized the commitment by the old and wise and kindled a spark within the young and impressionable. Congratulations on a job well done!

Appendix A
Geneological Information

When it is your turn to investigate forgotten branches of your family tree, and you have exhausted all of the knowledge of your family members, genealogical societies, such as the ones listed below, are excellent resources for helping you to dig deeper into your family's past. These societies have access to or are familiar with databases, records, and other sources of information that will help connect your family name to individuals across the country—and maybe across the world.

The Afro-American Historical and Genealogical Society (AAHGS) has many, active branches across the country.

Afro-American Historical and
  Genealogical Society, Inc.
  National Headquarters
P.O. Box 73086
Washington, D.C. 20056–3086

Arizona
AAHGS-Tucson
7739 East Broadway
Suite 195
Tucson, AZ 85710

**District of Columbia
  (Washington, DC)**
AAHGS-James Dent Walker
  Chapter, District of Columbia
P.O. Box 34683
Washington, DC 20043

Florida
AAHGS-Central Florida
P.O. Box 5742
Deltona, FL 32728

Illinois
AAHGS-Little Egypt
703 South Wall Street, #5
Carbondale, IL 62901

AAHGS-Patricia Liddell Researches
  Chicago Chapter
8829 South Merrill Street
Chicago, IL 60617

Maryland
AAHGS-Baltimore
P.O. Box 66265
Baltimore, MD 21218

AAHGS-Central Maryland
P.O. Box 2774
Columbia, MD 21045

Missouri
AAHGS-London Cheek Chapter,
  St. Louis
6514 Perry Court
St. Louis, MO 63121

New Jersey
AAHGS-New Jersey
18 Lindsley Avenue
Maplewood, NJ 07040

New York
AAHGS-Jean Sampson Scott
  Chapter, Greater New York Area
P.O. Box 022340
Brooklyn, NY 11202

Ohio
AAHGS-Cleveland Chapter
P.O. Box 200382
Cleveland, OH 44120–9998

Pennsylvania
AAHGS-Western Pennsylvania
1832 Runnette Street
Pittsburgh, PA 15235

Texas
AAHGS-Texas
7719 Wilmerdean Street
Houston, TX 77061

Virginia
AAHGS-Hampton Roads
P.O. Box 2448
Newport News, VA 23609

Other African American Genealogical Groups

California
California African American
  Genealogical Society
P.O. Box 8442
Los Angeles, CA 90008–0443

Georgia
African American Family History
  Association
P.O. Box 115268
Atlanta, GA 3031

Indiana
Indiana African American
  Historical and Genealogical
  Society
502 Clover Terace
Bloomington, IN 47404–1809

Michigan
Fred Hart Williams Genealogical
  Society
Detroit Public Library
5201 Woodward Avenue
Detroit, MI 48202

Pennsylvania
African American Genealogy
  Group
P.O. Box 1298
Philadelphia, PA 19105–1798

APPENDIX B

CITY BUREAUS AND TOURISM INFORMATION

This section provides a sample of local city bureaus and tourism offices—excellent resources for points of interest within your city. Brochures, discount tickets to local attractions, and maps are just some of the items available free of charge or at reduced rates. If you have scheduled a little free time in your reunion activities, let your family members roam at will.

Arizona
Office of Tourism
2702 North 3rd Street, Suite 4015
Phoenix AZ 85009
Telephone: (800) 842–8257
Web site: arizonaguide.com

Arizona Tourist Bureau
7000 N. 16th St. #120–237
Phoenix, Arizona 85020
Telephone: (602) 906–0005
Web site:
    webcreationsetc.com/Azguide

Arkansas
Arkansas Department of Parks and
    Tourism
One Capitol Mall
Little Rock, AR 72201
Telephone: (800) NATURAL

Fax: (501) 682–1364
E-mail: info@arkansas.com
Web site: arkansas.com

California
California Division of Tourism
Division of Tourism
    P.O. Box 1499
Sacramento, CA 95812
Telephone: (800) GO-CALIF
Web site: gocalif.ca.gov

Colorado
Colorado Tourism Board
P.O. Box 3524
Englewood, CO 80155
Telephone: (800) 265–6723

162

Connecticut

Connecticut Office of Tourism
Department of Economic and
    Community Development
505 Hudson Street
Hartford, CT 06106
Telephone: (800) CT-BOUND
 Web site: state.ct.us/tourism

Delaware

Delaware Tourism Office
99 Kings Highway
Dover, DE 19901
Telephone: (800) 441–8846
E-mail: dporter@state.de.us
Web site:
    state.de.us/tourism/intro.htm

Florida

Department of Commerce,
    Division of Tourism
126 West Van Buren
Tallahassee, FL 32399–2000
 Telephone: (888) 7-FLA-USA
Web site. flausa.com

Hawaii

Hawaii Visitors and Convention
    Bureau
2270 Kalakaua Ave., Suite 801
Honolulu, HI 96815
Telephone: (800) 353–5846
Fax: (808) 922–8991
Web site: visit.hawaii.org

Idaho

Idaho Recreation and Tourism
P.O. Box 83720
Boise, ID 83720–0093
Web site: visitid.org

Illinois

Illinois Bureau of Tourism
100 West Randolph Street,
    Suite 3–400
Chicago IL 60602

Indiana

Department of Commerce,
    Tourism Development Division
1 North Capitol, Suite 700
Indianapolis, IN 46204–2288
Telephone: (800) 291–8844
Fax: (317) 233–6887
Web site:
    state.in.us/tourism/index.html

Iowa

Department of Economic
    Development
Division of Tourism
200 East Grand Ave.
Des Moines, IA 50309
Telephone: (515) 242–4705
Web site:
    state.ia.us/tourism/index.html

Kansas

Kansas Department of Commerce
    and Housing Travel and
    Tourism Division
700 S.W. Harrison Street, #1300
Topeka, KS 66603–3712
Telephone: (800) 2KANSAS
Fax: (785) 296–5055

Kentucky

Kentucky Department of Travel
    Development
P.O. Box 2011
Frankfort, KY 40602

Telephone: (800) 225-TRIP
Fax: (502) 564–5695
Email: travel@exch.tour.state.ky.us
Web site: kentuckytourism.com

Louisiana
Office of Tourism
P.O. Box 94291
Baton Rouge, LA 70804–9291
Telephone: (800) 334–8626
Fax: (504) 342–8390

Maine
Maine Office of Tourism
Web site: visitmaine.com
The Maine Publicity Bureau Inc
P.O. Box 2300
325-B Water Street
Hallowell, Maine 04347–2300
Telephone: (800) 533–9595
Fax: (207) 623–0388
Web site: mainetourism.com

Maryland
Maryland Office of Tourism
  Development
217 East Redwood Street
Baltimore, MD 21202
Web site: mdisfun.org
Telephone: (800) MD-IS-FUN

Massachusetts
Berkshire Visitors Bureau
Telephone: (800) 237–5747

Michigan
P.O. Box 30226
Lansing, MI 48909

Telephone: (888) 78-GREAT
Fax: (517) 373–0059
E-mail: atwoodt@state.mi.us
Web site: travel-michigan.state.mi.us

Minnesota
Minnesota Office of Tourism
500 Metro Square
121 Seventh Place East
St. Paul, MN 55101–2112
Telephone: (800) 657–3700
Fax: (612) 296–7095
Web site: exploreminnesota.com

Mississippi
Mississippi Department of
  Economic and Community
  Development
Division of Tourism Development
P.O. Box 849
Jackson, MS 39205
Telephone: (601) 359–3297
Fax: (601) 359–5757
E-mail: tinquiry@mississippi.org
Web site:
  decd.state.ms.us/tourism.htm

Missouri
Division of Tourism
P.O. Box 1055, Truman State
  Office Bldg.
Jefferson City, MO 65102
Telephone: (800) 877–1234
E-mail: tourism@mail.state.mo.us
Web site: missouritourism.org

Montana
Travel Montana
P.O. Box 7549
Missoula, MT 59807

164

Telephone: (800) 847–4868
Fax: (406) 728–5713
Web site: travel.mt.gov

Nebraska
Nebraska Travel & Tourism Bureau
P.O. Box 98907
Lincoln, NE 68509–8907
Telephone: (800) 228–4307
    ext. 631
Fax: (402) 471–3026
E-mail:
    tourism@ded2.ded.state.ne.us
Web site: visitnebraska.org

Nevada
Nevada Commission on Tourism
Capitol Complex
Carson City, NV 89710
Telephone: (800) NEVADA–8
Fax: (702) 687–6779
Web site: travelnevada.com

New Hampshire
New Hampshire Office of Travel
    and Tourism Development
P.O. Box 1856
Concord NH 03302–1856
Telephone: (800) FUN-IN NH
Fax: (603) 271–6784
E-mail: visitnh@dred.state.nh.us
Web site: visitnh.gov

New Jersey
Department of Commerce and
    Economic Development
Division of Travel and Tourism

P.O. Box 826
Trenton, NJ 08625–0826
Telephone: (609) 633–2623
Fax: (609) 633–7418
E-mail: mbaugh@recom.com
Web site:
    state.nj.us/travel/index.html

New Mexico
Telephone: (800) SEE-NEWMEX
E-mail: enchantment@newmex-
    ico.org
Web site: newmexico.org

New York
Empire State Development
Travel Information Center
1 Commerce Plaza
Albany, NY 12245
Telephone: (800) CALL-NYS
Fax: (518) 486–6416
Web site: iloveny.state.ny.us

New York Convention & Visitors
    Bureau
Two Columbus Circle
New York, NY 10019
Telephone: (212) 484–1237
Fax: (212) 246–6310
Web site: nycvisit.com

North Carolina
Winston-Salem Convention and
    Visitors Bureau
P.O. Box 1408
Winston-Salem,
    North Carolina 27102

Telephone: (800) 331–7018
Fax: (910) 773–1404 or
  (800) WSNC CVB
Web site: winstonsalem.com

North Dakota
North Dakota Tourism Department
Liberty Memorial Building
604 East Boulevard
Bismarck, ND 58505
Telephone: (800) HELLO ND
 Fax: (701) 328–4878
Email:
  msmail.phertz@ranch.state.ND.US
Web site: ndtourism.com

Ohio
Ohio Division of Travel and
  Tourism
P.O. Box 1001, Columbus, OH
  43266–0101
Telephone: 800-BUCKEYE
Fax: (614) 466–6744
E-mail: ohiotourism@odod.ohio.gov
Web site: ohiotourism.com

Oklahoma
Oklahoma Tourism and Recreation
  Department
15 North Robinson, Room 801
P.O. Box 52002
Oklahoma City, OK 73152–2002
Telephone: (800) 652-OKLA
Fax: (405) 521–3992
Web site: otrd.state.ok.us

Oregon
Oregon Economic Development
  Department, Tourism Commission
775 Summer Street NE
Salem, OR 97310

Telephone: (800) 547–7842
Web site: traveloregon.com

Pennsylvania
Pennsylvania Office of Travel,
  Tourism, and Film
  Production
Room 400, Forum Building
Harrisburg, PA 17120
Telephone: (800) VISIT-PA
Fax: (717) 787–0687
E-mail:
  dcedtravel@dced.state.pa.us
Web site: state.pa.us/visit/

Rhode Island
Rhode Island Economic
  Development Corporation,
  Tourism Division
1 West Exchange Street
Providence, RI 02903
Telephone: (800) 556–2484
Fax: (401) 273–8270
Web site: visitrhodeisland.com

South Carolina
South Carolina Department of
  Parks, Recreation and Tourism
1205 Pendleton St.
Columbia, SC 29201–0071
Telephone: (800) 868–2492
Fax: (803) 734–0138

South Dakota
South Dakota Department of
  Tourism
711 East Wells Avenue
Pierre, SD 57501–3369
Telephone: (800) S-DAKOTA
Fax: (605) 773–3256

Tennessee
Tennessee Department of Tourist
  Development
320 6th Avenue North
Rachael Jackson Bldg.
5th floor
Nashville, TN 37202–3170
Telephone: (615) 741–2159
E-mail: tourdev@state.tn.us
Web site: state.tn.us/tourdev

Texas
Department of Commerce,
  Tourism Division
P.O. Box 12728
Austin, TX 78711
Telephone: (800) 8888-TEX
Web site: traveltex.com

Utah
The Utah Travel Council
Council Hall/Capitol Hill
Salt Lake City,
Utah 84114–1396
Telephone: (800) 200–1160
Fax: (801) 538–1399
Web site: utah.com

Vermont
Vermont Department of Tourism
  and Marketing
134 State Street Box 1471
Montpelier, VT 05601–1471
Telephone: (800) VERMONT
Fax: (802) 828–3233
Email:
  tourwebmaster@gate.dca.state.vt.us
Web site: travel-vermont.com

Virginia
Virginia Tourism Corporation
901 East Byrd Street
Richmond, VA 23219
Telephone: (800) VISIT-VA
Web site: virginia.org

Washington
Washington State Tourism Division
Web site: tourism.wa.gov

**Washington, District of
  Columbia**
D.C. Committee to Promote
  Washington
1212 New York Ave N.W. #600,
  Washington, DC 20005
Telephone: (800) 422–8644
Web site: washington.org

West Virginia
West Virginia Division of Tourism
2101 Washington St., E.
P.O. Box 50312
Charleston, WV 25305–0312
Telephone: (800) CALL-WVA
Web site:
  state.wv.us/tourism/default.htm

Wisconsin
Wisconsin Department of Tourism
201 West Washington Ave.
Madison, Wisconsin, 53702
Telephone: (800) 432-TRIP
E-mail:
  tourinfo@tourism.state.wi.us
Web site: tourism.state.wi.us

Wyoming

Division of Tourism and State
  Marketing
Interstate 25 at College Drive
Cheyenne, WY 82002
Telephone: (800) 225–5996
Fax: (307) 777–6904
Web site:
  commerce.state.wy.us/tourism

Virgin Islands

Virgin Islands Division of Tourism,
  St. Croix
Frederiksted
Custom House Bldg
Strand St
USVI 00840
Telephone: (809) 772–0357
Web site: usvi.net

Virgin Islands Division of Tourism,
  St. John
P.O. Box 200
Cruz Bay
St. John, VI 00831
Tel: (809) 776–6450

Virgin Islands Division of Tourism,
  St. Thomas
P.O. Box 6400
Charlotte Amalie
USVI 00830
Telephone: (809) 774–8784
Fax: (809) 774–4390